POPULISM
AND ELITISM

POPULISM AND ELITISM

POLITICS IN THE AGE OF EQUALITY

JEFFREY BELL

AdTI

An AdTI imprint book, sponsored in part
by the Alexis de Tocqueville Institution,
Arlington, Virginia

REGNERY GATEWAY
Washington, D.C.

Library of Congress Cataloging-In-Publication Data

Bell, Jeffrey, 1943–
    Populism and elitism : politics in the age of equality /
Jeffrey Bell.
        p.   cm.
    Includes bibliographical references and index
    ISBN 0-89526-517-6
    1. Democracy.   2. Populism.   3. Elite (Social sciences)
I. Title.
JC423.B3433   1992
321.8—dc20   91-47497
                                         CIP

Published in the United States by
Regnery Gateway
1130 17th Street, NW
Washington, DC 20036

Distributed to the trade by
National Book Network
4720-A Boston Way
Lanham, MD 20706

Printed on acid free paper

Manufactured in the United States of America

10   9   8   7   6   5   4   3   2   1

To Rosalie

ACKNOWLEDGMENTS

IN THE LATE 1970s I developed an interest in the subject of how and why countries adopt democracy and the factors that lead to their keeping it or not keeping it. I became convinced that, at least in the past few decades, the single biggest cause is the spread of belief in human equality, rather than advances in living standards, development of a broad middle class, or similar economic explanations.

Such economic factors were quite important in development of the *first* experiments with democratic institutions, in the ancient world and in places like the commercial city-states of medieval Europe, the Dutch Republic, England, France, and North America in more recent times. But my hypothesis was that once the institutions and techniques of mass democracy had been developed in these pioneer democracies, it became comparatively easy for less developed countries successfully to adopt democracy without an extended transition period. One of the implications was that in our post-monarchical and increasingly egalitarian-minded world, democracy was capable of spreading much more rapidly and widely than was commonly thought by students of this subject in the late 1970s and early 1980s.

As I began to contact people who had the ability to help me make this idea into a book, I received a somewhat surprising response. Virtually no one contested or questioned the thesis directly. Rather, the predominant reaction was one of apathy or indifference to the possibility of an increasingly democratic world. Neither was it that anyone opposed the *desirability* of democracy in more and more countries, or argued that this development would be premature at least for some of those countries. They tended to accept my emphasis on the importance of the spread of egalitarian belief (at least for sake of argument) and even mildly welcomed the more democratic world it implied, but expressed pessimism about what newly enfranchised electorates would do with their power once attained.

I found this kind of pessimism about people's political ability among elites of the Right (my own background), the Left, and the moderate center. It was almost as if this pessimism about people was part of being a well-educated, well-regarded person—that is, part of elite status itself.

Aided by some generous foundation grants and hospitality from a number of universities and scholarly institutes, I plowed ahead for several years on my research on the making of modern mass democracy. But as the writing began to flow in the 1980s, I found the book heading in different directions. Though some of the original material remains relevant and remains in the book, much more had to be put on the shelf.

It isn't that I thought the spread of democracy a less interesting or less important subject, merely that I might have more of interest to say if I changed my emphasis toward a discussion of the role of optimism or pessimism about people in countries in which political equality had already triumphed.

Defining these two things as populism and elitism is not conventional, and involves using them to apply to political leaders and thinkers who never used and in some cases never heard these terms. I am equally well aware that the terms populism and elitism are often used in a very different sense, more or less as identifications of class origin or allegiance, or even (in the case of populism) as a description of political tactics.

The fact remains that optimism or pessimism about people's ability exists in everyone, at least as an intuitive part of how one looks at the world. Since the book's thesis is that this factor is the most important thing to know about modern democratic politics, single words are at least highly desirable for the purpose of the book's discussions. It is in part because they have so often been used in different contexts that I begin the book by trying to define the two words carefully in the sense I understand them.

Once established not as descriptions of class orientation or political tactics but as distinct viewpoints, populism and elitism cast light, I believe, on a whole series of topics not easily explained otherwise. Why do most articulate people prefer tax breaks for corporations to personal rate reduction? What is it that explains widespread dislike by elites of 30-second political commercials on television? Why has a Republican hammerlock on the presidency co-existed with Democratic control of all other levels of government for a full generation? Why did a liberal like Robert Kennedy do so well among voters who were simultaneously attracted to George Wallace and Richard Nixon? What is it about political novices as different as Woodrow Wilson and Ronald Reagan that enabled them to leapfrog entire generations of better-trained politicians?

Perhaps the best test of an analytical tool is whether it helps elucidate the events one has experienced at first hand. In the 1960s, a period that bulks large in the book, I found myself as an undergraduate at a politically quickening Columbia until 1965; as a U.S. army enlisted man stationed in Vietnam's Mekong Delta during the Tet offensive in the early days of February 1968; and by October of that same year, on the Nixon campaign plane preparing the candidate's daily news summary as his seemingly insurmountable lead over Hubert Humphrey melted away.

In the two decades that followed, I immersed myself in national and state politics, serving in three additional presidential campaigns and making two unsuccessful U.S. Senate races of my own. As an issue advisor to Ronald Reagan in 1976, I landed in the middle of controversy by persuading Reagan to advocate a $90-billion program of government decentralization and tax cuts. After his defeat to Gerald Ford, I went to New Jersey and challenged liberal Republican Senator Clifford Case as an early advocate of the Kemp-Roth 30 percent tax cut plan. I upset Case in June 1978, but lost the general election to the Democratic nominee, Bill Bradley.

In 1980, I wrote seven issue-oriented television commercials for the Reagan presidential campaign. The commercials, which centered on advocacy of federal tax cuts, were aired in the month leading up to the New Hampshire primary and were used in the rest of the primary states. During the Reagan presidency I was heavily involved in the battles for the tax cut of 1981 and the Tax Reform Act of 1986, in the latter working closely with Congressman Jack Kemp and Senators Bill Bradley and Bob Packwood. In 1988 I was national coordinator of Kemp's presidential campaign.

In applying what Michael Barone calls the "lens" of populism-elitism analysis to these two decades of political and policy experience, I found my view of what had been happening taking on a very different context and meaning. Right, left, and center, though by no means drained of all significance, began to recede in importance as an explanation of the political battles I had lived through. I would like to think this lens can perform a comparable service in analyzing not just the recent past and other chunks of political history, but providing the reader with a useful guide to the age of political equality that is just beginning to unfold in the world of the 1990s.

I would like to thank the Eagleton Institute of Politics at Rutgers University, the Lehrman Institute, and the American Enterprise Institute for their generosity in providing the opportunity for much of my research. Particularly helpful were Alan Rosenthal at Eagleton, William Baroody and William Schneider at AEI, and Nicholas Rizopolous and Robert Tucker at Lehrman. Mr. Rizopolous was cogent and persuasive in guiding me toward the essay format that brought the book within a realistic compass. Mr. Tucker gave valuable advice on previous writings on democratic culture and philosophy. I owe Mr. Schneider much for heightening my awareness of the importance of values issues in American political history.

Among those providing generous support were the Lehrman Institute, the John M. Olin Foundation, the Allen-Bradley Foundation, the W. H. Brady Foundation, Richard and Virginia Gilder, Neil Gagnon, John Holman, Robert Perry, and, above all, the

Reader's Digest Foundation, which sponsors the DeWitt Wallace Chair I occupied for more than a year at AEI. I owe a special debt of gratitude to Kenneth Tomlinson and William Schulz of the *Digest* not only for the Foundation's backing, but for their friendship and encouragement throughout this project.

Jude Wanniski first persuaded me to write a book about politics, and Irving Kristol built my confidence in moving ahead with the framework established in the early chapters. Robert Novak provided important ideas and structural suggestions. Leslie Lenkowsky and Ralph Benko also deserve warm thanks for their help and friendship.

Jacob van Rossum was an indefatigable and enthusiastic research assistant. Mac Carey and Dennis Teti found time in their busy schedules to contribute research and ideas. Robert Weiss donated countless hours of computer work inputting and updating the text as it developed.

I owe a great deal to the Alexis de Tocqueville Institution and its chairman, Gregory Fossedal, for their sponsorship of the book. No one could ask for a more supportive publisher than Alfred Regnery and his team at Regnery Gateway. In particular, Trish Bozell deserves many thanks for her shrewd editing.

I would be remiss if I did not mention three highly valued friends who are also my business partners. Lewis Lehrman helped in as many ways as was possible—with ideas, generous help in gaining financial support, and warm encouragement. John Mueller provided keen insight into economic and other issues that figure in the book's analysis. And Frank Cannon contributed vast patience and penetrating insight to help me write the closing chapters.

Finally, my wife Rosalie O'Connell was my loving partner and thoughtful critic without whom the book would never have been written.

CONTENTS

PREFACE

BY MICHAEL BARONE
Co-Author, *The Almanac of American Politics*

WE THE PEOPLE are the first three words of the Constitution of the United States. They seem a curious choice to those still influenced by the thesis, disproved by later historians but disseminated through a host of secondary sources, that the framers of the Constitution were rich creditors bent on increasing their net worth. But for those with ears for what Lincoln called "the mystic chords of memory" they ring true. The elite who created the government of the United States believed that they could speak legitimately only in the name of a people each individual of whom was putatively equal. (Of course for the Framers the people consisted of only white males; the inclusion of others under this happily elastic term would take time and bloodshed, but would happen.) The framers understood that the offices in any government must of necessity be filled by an elite. But they also sensed that government must in important ways be responsive to the people. They built into the politics of our country, and hence of the dozens of countries that have followed our example over the last two hundred years, a tension between elite and public opinion which is sometimes greater, sometimes lesser, but never entirely absent.

That tension is the subject, broadly speaking, of Jeffrey Bell's

Populism and Elitism: Politics in the Age of Equality. Bell recognizes of course that by definition those who govern or seek to are an elite. But he makes a useful division of the political world between those who on balance trust elite opinion and those who on balance trust popular opinion. Sometimes, as he points out, there is no great gulf between the two. In the 1950s, for example, elite and popular opinion roughly coincided on issues of economics, foreign policy, and cultural values, with just enough differences to fuel the competition between two political parties and allied large economic units—big corporations and big labor unions—who had inherited regional, ethnic, and cultural constituencies from earlier, more hotly contested political conflicts. But sometimes the gulf can be very wide indeed. Consider what became one of the most resounding issues of the 1988 presidential campaign. The accurate charge by George Bush's campaign that Michael Dukakis favored, articulately and in the midst of controversy over a period of eleven years, a policy of allowing weekend furloughs for prisoners sentenced to life imprisonment without parole, influenced opinion in Bush's favor with a very large majority of voters. Yet articulate elites, especially in the news media, viewed the issue as illegitimate, even though no rational argument whatever can be made in support of Dukakis's position.

Populism and Elitism helps answer two questions most American historians and political writers have left unaddressed and propounds a third which every serious thinker about these things ought to ponder. The first of these questions was raised by James Q. Wilson in his review in *The New Republic* of my own 1990 book *Our Country: The Shaping of America from Roosevelt to Reagan.* Why, Wilson asked, did the liberal American elite, which seemed so confident of its own policies and of the basic goodness of our system of governance at the beginning of the 1960s, turn so violently against it in the years centering on 1967 and 1968? Bell identifies the same turn in elite thought: "Around 1967, the balance among powerful political and journalistic elites began to tip toward the views of society's harshest critics." And he suggests its causes by putting the events of these years in narrative context. He shows how the settling of the once hotly contested issues of how to respond to the Depression and fight the Cold War left the field open for conflicts over values issues. He shows how the otherwise almost entirely benign civil rights revolution raised questions in the minds of elites about the equality and fairness of other institutions, questions that had the malign effect of casting a pall of illegitimacy over the whole society. He shows how disappointment over John Kennedy's record and the shock of his assassination and how the response to the Vietnam War—so different from the response to the arguably similar war in Korea a dozen years before—undermined belief in liberal governance. The liberal elites, so smug and confident at the beginning of the decade, turned their face away from events that were in most cases the consequences of their own acts and found fault with the larger society instead.

This culminated in the single year of 1968, to which, as Bell brilliantly points out, the elite and the people responded in entirely different ways to one horrifying event after another—the Tet offensive, the murders of Martin Luther King and Robert Kennedy, the campus rebellions like Columbia's and black riots like Washington's, the disorders at the Democrats' Chicago convention. To these events the response of most Americans was for government to shoulder what is always its first responsibility, to provide a stable and predictable order within which ordinary people can lead their personal and professional lives. The response of the preponderance of the elite was to embrace the values of articulate protesters and to see the desire for "law and order"—a phrase first put into the political dialogue by Robert Kennedy, then picked up on by Richard Nixon—as a form of racism morally akin to Bull Connor's police dogs and firehoses. In policy terms, their response was the Kerner Commission report, published amid the post-Tet turmoil in March 1968, which urged a massive increase in the public sector, a guaranteed income, and racial quotas and preferences—all remedies massively rejected, then and ever since, by the large majority of American voters.

"The partisan upheaval of 1968—rooted in simultaneous and cross-cutting realignments in the elite and popular opinion streams—would prove far from temporary," Bell writes. Richard Nixon's apparent attempt to fuse them by embracing the elite policies of Harvard professors Henry Kissinger and Daniel Patrick Moynihan failed to propitiate his political enemies, and the disgraceful end of his administration enabled the elite to think that it could command national allegiance. The repudiation of the Carter administration's economic and foreign policies in the election of 1980 did not much dent that perception.

Which leads to the second largely unaddressed question which Bell answers: Why has the liberal elite totally failed to acknowledge the successes of Ronald Reagan and his policies? For by the standards these liberals themselves apply to, for example, the administrations of Franklin Roosevelt and John Kennedy, those successes are undoubted. The Reagan economic policies led to eight years of low-inflation economic growth, a record never before achieved in American history. The Reagan foreign policies led to a total American victory in the Cold War and the end of communism and the Soviet Union. Strong arguments can be made in each case that these successes are the proximate result of these policies; yet the liberal elite, especially in the press, treats them as simply happy accidents—a classic example of people who think of themselves as open-minded having minds that are totally closed. The reason, Bell says, is that what these people care most about are values, and on values issues they are in many ways winning. Moral relativism and equality of result have become the guiding values of public schools and universities—with the result, Bell might have added, of falling intellectual achievement—of the news media, and even of leaders of large institutions like corporations and churches. Put together, these two values produce regimes like that of Sweden's—with a welfare state so all-embracing that the family is withering away— or the Politically Correct campuses of America of the late 1980s, which in the name of "diversity" insist on a stultifying uniformity of opinion and belief.

That suggests the question Bell leaves us to ponder. Will the cultural values of the American elite, frozen in amber since the *annus horribilis* of 1968, squander the success that American foreign and economic policies have won and are continuing to win all over the world? Bell leaves us with the picture of an American elite so desperate to hold onto the illusion of its own moral superiority that it stubbornly ignores and distorts what is going on in the world around it that a happy answer to this question is not at all certain. I admit to greater optimism. In the last dozen years, ideas of personal restraint have gained ground against the late 1960s' preoccupation with liberation, and the practical consequences of the fusion of moral relativism and equality-of-results, when placed under the spotlight, are soundly rejected even by intended beneficiaries, in Sweden and on American campuses and, in the case of racial preferences, among Americans black and Hispanic and Asian. The younger generation of Americans, those now under thirty, perceive a connection between effort and reward and, as those left untended by absent parents and uneducated by liberal-run schools in the age of liberation, are determined to repair the damage they have seen in their own lives. Even the long split-level realignment—the Republican hold on the presidency and Democratic hold on Congress—stands to be altered, in my view, in 1992 and through the 1990s. But these remain open questions. What Bell has done in *Populism and Elitism* is to give us a lens through which to see them and through which to make sense of the last twenty-five years of our political history.

POPULISM
AND ELITISM

INTRODUCTION

Populism is optimism about people's ability to make decisions about their lives.

Elitism is optimism about the decision-making ability of one or more elites, acting on behalf of other people.

Populism implies pessimism about an elite's ability to make decisions for the people affected.

Elitism implies pessimism about the people's ability to make decisions affecting themselves.

The argument between populism and elitism has become the most important one in politics today. Not only does it explain more of what is happening in the world than the usual distinctions between left and right or socialism and capitalism; it extends in one form or another into virtually every area of human life.

For most of the five thousand years of recorded civilization, this argument was not so important, for until as recently as 1775, the world was almost wholly monarchical. Although experimentation with a narrowly based parliamentary government had been going on for more than a century in the British monarchy, it is fair to say that no country larger than a city-state had ever been able to maintain an independent democracy or republic for very long. Republics that expanded beyond their city limits had rarely granted voting rights to people in conquered territories, and republics such as Rome that became empires eventually saw the collapse of popular institutions

3

even at home. In 1775, most political theorists thought democracy in a territory larger than a city-state impossible.

In the world of monarchy that prevailed for most of known history, the competence of people was no more than a secondary issue, because people were subjects. They belonged to a king or to a nobleman or to both. They were part of a realm. People may have made many decisions affecting their lives, but on a matter in which the monarch had a concern, the question of competence did not often arise. The people were his to direct.

Today, only three or four countries, mostly in the Arab world, could be described as ruling monarchies. The Western idea of political equality is universal. Few voices can be heard, at least for the record, disagreeing with the idea of government *for* the people.

This is why it is here, in a world of political equality, that elitist views become important. Since today it is no longer easy to deny people control over their lives, as in feudalism or slavery, the only *effective* argument for decisions by an elite on behalf of other people is the elitist argument that such a decision would be better for the people—that is, pessimism about the people's ability to make decisions affecting themselves.

In this egalitarian climate, the growth of populist belief in people's competence is often the last step toward democracy. Since government *for* the people gives people equal standing in political society, growth in optimism about their political competence makes adoption of government *by* the people more and more likely.

But closely related as the populist-elitist argument is to the growth of democracy, it is important to understand that a trend toward populism does not make democracy inevitable—only much more likely—and that adoption of democracy does not end the argument between populism and elitism. This is because the argument between populism and elitism is usually one of practicality rather than of moral absolutes.

In the later monarchical period, a populist who was also a monarchist might be optimistic about the people's ability to make policy decisions, yet oppose it because of a belief that these decisions belong to the king *by right*. But this would not necessarily paralyze his advocacy. This monarchical populist might try to persuade the king to delegate the decision that was his by right to his subjects, on the *practical* ground that their decision was likely to be better than the king's.

In more recent times, an elitist might be pessimistic about the people's ability to make decisions on a matter of public policy affecting them, and still favor popular decision-making on that issue. In this case, the democratic elitist might try to persuade the people to delegate a decision that is theirs by right to an elite, on the *practical* ground that the decision of the elite is likely to be better than what the people would decide if left to themselves.

In fact, it is precisely in a transition between monarchy and democracy that one would expect to see these two "hybrid" types—the populistic monarchist and the democratic elitist—playing prominent roles. To take one such transition, the American Revolution, we in fact find defenders of monarchy like Edmund Burke advocating increased "home rule" for the North American and other British colonies, and advocates of republicanism like George Washington expressing pessimism about the people's ability to make decisions for themselves. But once a transition from monarchy to democracy is made, populism gains at least a rhetorical upper hand, if only because it is hard to win popular majorities while expressing open pessimism about the voters themselves.

But no one should think that elites are incapable of sincere populist beliefs. The spread of optimism about people in the upper classes of North America and France were key preconditions for the American and French Revolutions. The argument between populism and elitism is a disagreement about the competence of people to handle their affairs, not a form of class conflict. A member of a political elite may be a populist; and a member of the lower-middle class may have elitist views.

A great deal of political philosophy and political science deals with the relationship between the rulers and the ruled. But as a society moves toward democracy and equality replaces subordination, persuasion replaces command, and it becomes less helpful to think of society in those terms. To the extent that self-government advances, public opinion and the shaping of it become the preoccupation of elites and would-be elites.

In modern mass democracy, elites exist, indeed they multiply as society becomes richer and more complex. Each elite has its own pattern of belief; taken together they represent the elite opinion stream. The people who are part of this status-based opinion stream have enormous contact and interaction with the popular opinion stream. But the predominant thrust of elite opinion may or may not be successful in influencing popular opinion at any given time, or on any given issue. In other words, the course of public opinion depends on the interaction between the elite opinion stream and popular opinion stream, but these two opinion streams are independent and at times seem as likely to clash as to intersect.

In the 1960s, it is clear that they were moving in opposite directions. In 1960, student polls on the eight Ivy League campuses—a reasonably good reflection of the elite opinion stream—found majorities for Richard Nixon on six of eight campuses (the exceptions were Columbia and Harvard, Kennedy's alma mater). The country went narrowly Democratic.

In 1968, Hubert Humphrey won overwhelmingly on the Ivy League campuses over the same Republican nominee, Richard Nixon. On some campuses, Nixon received fewer votes than did minor-party candidates. Meanwhile, the nation was swinging narrowly Republican.

In 1960, the 17th Congressional ("Silk Stocking") District on the East Side of Manhattan, a bastion of elite opinion, went solidly for Nixon. In 1968, with the nation voting the other way, the 17th was overwhelmingly for Humphrey.

To repeat: popular opinion does not at all times have a leaning toward populism (i.e., optimism about people's ability to handle their own affairs). Elite opinion does not always have a leaning toward elitism (i.e., optimism about the ability of elites to make decisions on behalf of the people). But it stands to reason that during those times when this *is* true, the tension between elites and society as a whole, never wholly absent, sharpens in intensity, and the argument between populism and elitism gains an unpleasant edge on both sides. In the United States and most other democracies, the present is such a time.

CHAPTER 1

THE AGE OF EQUALITY

THE MEANING OF monarchy is political elevation by right. Thus, even though there is more than one kind of equality, the victory of equality over monarchy since 1775 is first and foremost the victory of *political* equality.

Monarchy of course had implications for religion, economics, and all other areas of human life. But at its most sacerdotal (the priest-kings of ancient Mesopotamia) and at its most material (mercantilism), monarchy was never other than a system of political mastery. A king might act for religious or economic ends, but his acts were political.

In the world of equality, no one has political mastery over anyone else by right. Such mastery must be won by persuasion in the democratic world, and justified in the name of equality elsewhere.

The idea of political equality has become the most widely accepted value on earth. Thus, since the most tangible form of political equality is voting, the most repressive regime feels the need to hold sham elections, or to promise free ones in the future.

As the 1980s wore on, more and more of the countries that had seen only sham elections found themselves holding real ones. In Latin America, dictatorships of the Left and Right disappeared one by one, to the point where in 1990 Cuba was the only full-fledged dictatorship left in the Western Hemisphere. By 1980, all governments in Western Europe had become democratic for the first time in history. By 1990 they had been joined by all of Eastern Europe except for Albania and parts of Yugoslavia. Early that same year, the Soviet Union itself had taken the crucial step toward multi-party elections by removing the Communist party's monopoly on power. By August 1991, the Communist party was illegal. In most of Asia and Africa the trend was not as striking, but more and more of these countries seemed poised to join the trend in the 1990s.

Not all of these gains by democratic forces, of course, will prove permanent. But in 1990, in sharp contrast to 1890, political equality seemed a worldwide principle that had little or no *ideological* opposition. Even where there was opposition, hardly anyone questioned directly the *desirability* of political equality, and the few significant politicians who did (such as the rulers of Saudi Arabia) had an air of anachronism about them.

Indeed, one of the last significant *avowed* opponents of political equality, Francisco Franco, provides an ironic instance of its unassailability. His attempt to restore the House of Bourbon to succeed him came to grief when his chosen anti-egalitarian instrument, King Juan Carlos, let his kingly powers lapse and became Spain's most effective champion of democracy.

The widespread, nearly universal advocacy of political equality is often seen as a sign of the ease with which it can safely be ignored in practice. Yet even from a practical point of view, it is hard to see how embracing a concept is the most effective way of crushing it. At the very least, the idea is kept alive by the very people who privately despise it. They would be unlikely to pay it lip service unless they sensed overt opposition to political equality was fruitless in the twentieth century.

But within that broad agreement, there is still the question of whether political equality is a fact or a goal. Almost all regimes agree that equality is desirable, but is it something that exists, and needs to be embodied, *now*, or is it something that has to wait until some time in the future?

This tug between present and future egalitarianism splits along populist-elitist lines. The populist, a believer in the ability of people to handle their own affairs better than an elite, will tend to believe in *present* equality. The elitist, with his optimism about the superior ability of elites to handle people's affairs, will tend to believe in *future* equality.

To put it another way, the egalitarian populist believes political equality is something that exists and must guide political life because it is *innate*. The egalitarian elitist believes that political equality is a desirable end to be worked toward under the leadership of elites who believe it can and should be achieved. The egalitarian elitist, pessimistic about most people's ability to make political decisions in the present, believes in managing *toward* equality. By definition, managed equality requires some kind of elite to do the managing.

Populism's belief in present or innate equality does not mean that each voter has exactly the same ability as every other, or even that every group within the electorate is roughly equal to every other in level of education or political sophistication. But it does believe in the competence of the electorate to handle its own affairs *relative to the competence of elites*. For groups within the electorate that lack present competence relative to other groups, egalitarian populists tend to believe in what might be called psychological populism: that is, that rough political equality is best obtained by giving such groups equal political status now, rather than consigning them, explicitly or tacitly, to guidance by a more knowledgeable elite. Populists are optimistic about an electorate's ability to learn by doing.

Egalitarian elitists often believe that the granting of present political equality is an empty gesture in the absence of other kinds of equality. Few Marxists, for example, would disagree that equality is an ultimate value in politics. But most would argue that real political equality is impossible unless economic equality has been achieved first, through the guidance of an ideological elite.

In the democratic world, egalitarian elitists would not deny the people their right to vote, but would tend to be pessimistic about the people's ability to make proper use of this right in the absence of simultaneous steps toward managed equality in the political realm and in other areas. For example, in the United States many advocates of managed equality favor not only the granting of black voting rights, but court intervention in reapportionment decisions to ensure equality of *result* in the political process. In most cases, this is a reflection of elitist pessimism about the ability of blacks to fend for themselves in a regime of pure political equality. In the interest of future equality, they would legislate present favoritism.

For obvious reasons, there is often great ideological tension within a person who believes that elitism is necessary to achieve equality. The two most radically egalitarian communist leaders of this century, Stalin and Mao, were at periodic war with their own ruling Communist parties. Stalin killed a generation of communist leaders, while Mao killed some, purged others, and sent many more to the fields to purge them of elitism.

In retrospect, the death of Mao and the fall of his allies, the Gang of Four, in 1976 may have proved a decisive turning point in the history not just of communism but of equality. That event ended the last serious effort to implement the Stalinist-Maoist vision of equality of *economic* result in the world of Marxism. With the end of that effort, as Mao appears to have sensed, communism itself had little remaining ideological legitimacy in the age of equality and its decline was likely to be rapid.

The truly radical view of equality—namely, that it is innate in human beings and exists right now—has its roots in Hebrew, classical (particularly Stoic), and Christian thought, and was fully believed by the founders of modern political theory, including Locke, Montesquieu, and Rousseau. Their view is reflected in the American Declaration of Independence's contention that all men are *created* equal.

Not all believers in innate equality believe it is God-given, and none believes that it involves equal abilities by all people in all spheres. Equality is not uniformity or identity. In the words of the political philosopher Carl Cohen, "It is, simply, that beneath all the undeniable differences among men there is in every human being an element or aspect, or essential quality which justifies our treating him as the equal of every other in the largest sphere of human life."

Cohen goes on to quote Immanuel Kant on the difference between possessing value and possessing dignity: "Whatever has a value can be replaced by something else which is *equivalent* in value; whatever, on the other hand, is above all value, and therefore admits of no equivalent, has a dignity." And Cohen concludes: "[S]ome things in the world cannot be measured on any scale of values; they are invaluable, priceless. That is the case with every human being. . . . Every man has a life to lead; it is a life unique, irreplaceable, having dignity but no price. In living such a life all men are equal, and that is why they have, every single one, an equal stake in the decisions of the community whose general purpose is the protection and improvement of its members. In summary, the special and inclusive nature of the political community gives to every man an equal concern in the outcome of its decisions."[1]

The use of the word "priceless" sums up the populist view of equality. However unequal people may be in their various capacities, the pricelessness of each, and the equal stake of each in the outcome of politics, puts their equality on a higher plane and makes it unassailable. Only the more pessimistic view of political equality, that it is not innate and can be achieved only by management, can justify domination by an elite.

Elitists are pessimistic about equality because they believe present inequality so severe that only management by political elites can achieve equality in the future. Populists are optimistic about equality because they regard each human being as having a unique dignity that is in the present tense and must therefore be embodied in politics.

At least since 1945, the argument over the nature of equality has dominated global politics, not only as an argument between democracy and one-party socialism, but within virtually every democracy and dictatorship as well. On its resolution hinges the future of a newly kingless humanity.

CHAPTER 2

THE FRUITS OF LABOR

ECONOMIC POPULISM is optimism about people's ability to make economic decisions affecting their lives. Economic elitism believes in the superiority of decisions by one or more elites acting on behalf of the people in economic matters. Elitist economic intervention can occur at any or all three stages of the economic life of people: in work, in the consumption of the product of work, and in the accumulation and handling by people of that part of work's product not immediately consumed—that is, of property.

Arguments between populism and elitism in economics have therefore tended to focus on the role of people as workers, as consumers, and as holders of property. The optimistic outlook of populism in these areas is associated with three doctrines: the labor theory of value, consumer sovereignty, and universal (popular) property rights. *

* The statement of the labor theory of value appears as the first sentence of Adam Smith's *The Wealth of Nations*: "The annual labour of every nation is the fund which originally supplies it with all the necessaries and conveniences of life which it annually consumes, and which consist always either in the immediate produce of that labour, or in what is purchased with that produce from other nations." Also: "Labour alone, therefore, never varying in its own value, is alone the ultimate and real standard by which the value of all commodities can at all times be estimated and compared."

The theory of consumer sovereignty, as defined in the *McGraw-Hill Dictionary of Eco-*

Because modern society has many elites, economic elitism comes in more than one form, and one kind of elitism may disagree strongly with another. A conservative elitist might feel that economic decisions are superior when made by an economic elite he calls "capital" or "management," while an economic elitist of more liberal views might feel the decisions could be better made by government elites. But the two kinds of elites would agree in their pessimism about the ability of most people to make economic decisions affecting themselves.

Adam Smith, the founder of modern economics, was suspicious of both governmental and non-governmental elites, and particularly of the frequent collaboration he saw between the two. Writing against the reigning doctrine of mercantilism, which defined a nation's wealth in terms of its holdings of gold and silver generated by its trade surplus, he fixed the origin of wealth in human labor and ingenuity.

As with political populism, economic populism becomes more important as monarchy gives way to equality. If the king "owned" the people in a political sense, he even more clearly was the owner of the land they worked on and the production they were able to bring out of it. It is no accident that the rise of the Dutch Republic in the seventeenth century and the curbing of monarchy in England in the second half of that century coincided with the beginnings of the modern growth economy and the first serious elaboration of private (that is, popular) property rights. Property rights existed under monarchy, but only one person (the monarch) enjoyed them fully. Even most noblemen lacked the ultimate title to their land enjoyed by small farmers in certain regimes of political equality, such as the United States.

At the same time, a gradual change took place in the attitude to work itself. In the age of monarchy, work had little prestige in the

---

nomic Theory, supports "the dominant role of consumers in determining types and quantities of goods purchased by an economic system. . . . Each consumer purchase is actually the casting of 'dollar votes' by which consumers can register their desires in terms of goods and services, which translates directly into business profits. As consumer demand increases, production of these goods is increased to take advantage of new profit potential."

royal and noble circles that controlled society. Work was something done *for* the monarch or the noble by clerks, tenant farmers, or other people controlled by the political elites. Even commerce, increasingly lucrative for a few families as the Middle Ages in Europe wore on, was considered beneath contempt, or at best a necessary evil, by king and nobility.

Only with the spread of belief in equality, and a corresponding decline of belief in rule by blood elites, could human labor begin to acquire dignity. Political ownership of the bodies of people, whether through feudalism or the extreme form of slavery, implied as well an ownership of any product of their labor. Optimism about people's economic ability might exist in a few circles, but it hardly mattered as long as the political elite claimed ownership or control of people's bodies, and therefore of work, consumption, and property.

Just as political populism—a practical opinion about people's ability to govern themselves—and the belief in political equality— an essentially moral view of people's rights—aided and abetted each other without being the same thing, so the concept of economic populism and such moral beliefs as the rights of labor and property often sprang up in the same eras and in the same thinkers. In the seventeenth century, John Locke not only propounded popular property rights and an early version of the labor theory of value, but he also believed that the institution of these ideas as the guiding principles of government would cause people so to multiply wealth as to render the wealth they started with "almost worthless" by comparison. A century later, Adam Smith predicted that the growing trend toward division of labor would enable people to produce more and more effectively, vastly increasing the wealth of the masses.

Smith founded the free-market school that dominated nineteenth-century economic thought, but in one crucial respect—his belief in the economic competence of common people and thus in their ability to generate broad-based economic growth—he had few successors. Economic thought quickly drifted into a view of economics as a self-contained area of life whose natural state was "equilibrium," or no growth. "The economist traditionally," writes Peter Drucker, "until well past World War II . . . took it for granted that economic resources are given and limited, so that the problem is their most effective distribution in a system of equilibrium. In this respect Keynes, however much he otherwise might have differed from his predecessors, was as traditional as anyone. It was not until the most recent decades, until the advent of 'economic development' as a goal of economic policy— with President Truman's 'Point Four' declaration of the early 1950s being the crucial date—that proper economists accepted the purposeful creation of dynamic disequilibrium as possible and meaningful."[2]

Much more typical of the emerging profession of economics than Adam Smith was the English clergyman Thomas Malthus, who believed that as population increased, consumption would inevitably outpace production, leading to mass starvation. This profound pessimism about the mass of people as economic actors shapes much of economic and social thought in the elite opinion stream even today. One of the few populist economists of the nineteenth century, Henry George, wrote that Malthus's fundamental mistake was to analyze human beings as if they were animals.

But the fact remained that just as the rise of political equality implied broad-based economic growth as a desirable *goal* of politics, so the simultaneous rise of optimism about people implied broad-based economic growth as a realistic *possibility* for society. Thus, however few successors Smith's optimism had in the profession of economics itself, it is not surprising that economic growth became a central *political* issue in those countries where equality was winning and electorates were growing.

Indeed, *The Wealth of Nations* became the bible of a century of practicing politicians in the small, mostly English-speaking world of nineteenth-century democracy. Figures such as Jefferson, Jackson, Martin Van Buren, and Samuel Tilden in the United States; George Brown in Canada; and Robert Peel and William Gladstone in Britain, were devoted readers of Smith and believed the key to prosperity was the energizing of common people and the limiting of elite influence in economic life.

As Robert Kelley's *The Transatlantic Persuasion: The Liberal-Democratic Mind in the Age of Gladstone* makes clear, the nineteenth-century economic debate can be seen in large measure as a disagreement between populist and elitist visions of economic life.[3] Once Gladstone had led the Peelite faction of the Conservatives into the Liberal party in the 1850s, the argument was almost exclusively along party lines. The Liberals in Britain and Canada, and the Democrats in the United States, took the populist view, while the Conservatives in Britain and Canada, and the Federalists, Whigs, and Republicans in the United States—represented by such figures as Hamilton, Clay, Disraeli, and John A. Macdonald in Canada—took the elitist view. This view featured, among other things, a close quasi-mercantilist partnership between entrepreneurs and government; a strong belief in protective tariffs; an affirmative position on central banking and paper money, sometimes verging into inflationism; and support for public-works spending by government on the model of Henry Clay's American System.

The Liberal-Democratic tradition in the three countries, by contrast, supported popular property rights (including bargain-basement land sales) and the unlimited right of anyone to incorporate; a strict separation of government from business interests; strong opposition to manipulative central banking and support for the international gold standard and free trade. These parties championed the interest of the consumer, the small farmer, and the small businessman, and in cultural terms they represented the "out groups" of the three societies, such as the French in Canada, the Irish in America, and the Dissenters in Britain.

In periods when elections were fought out mainly on economic issues, populist parties were successful not only in winning elections, but in igniting dramatic economic growth. One thinks particularly of the years of growth that attended the Gladstone ministries in Britain and those that followed the final victory of the Jackson

Democrats over the Whigs on economic issues in the 1840s and 1850s. But in the United States, the Democrats got on the wrong side of the slavery issue (which was so much more than economic) and because of the resistance of the unelected House of Lords, Gladstone's half-century era of dominance went aground on the issue of Irish Home Rule.

With the fall of Gladstone in 1894, an era in British political and economic life came to an end. From his first major appointment, as president of the board of trade in the Peel cabinet in 1843, Gladstone and his ideas had dominated economic policy-making for more than half a century. His optimism about people's economic ability led him to make repeated cuts in taxes, tariffs, and government budgets never matched by any political leader before or since, and the productive record of the British nation in those years rewarded his faith.

But Gladstone was to have no successor, at least in his own country. British politics after 1894 reverted to its normal rhythm of aristocratic elitism—an intense class consciousness that saw little optimism about people among the political elites of the Right or the Left.

In the United States, Democrats after 1860 were a minority party for the first time in the century, but the Adam Smith tradition stayed alive in such figures as Samuel Tilden, one of Andrew Jackson's economic advisors who lived to become a tax-cutting reform governor of New York and a near-president in the election of 1876, and Woodrow Wilson, whose political inspiration was Gladstone and who brought his brand of populism briefly onto the global stage. But the deflationary agricultural crisis of the 1880s and 1890s generated a split between rural and urban populists (the rural wing taking the name for the first time), and the Republicans under Mark Hanna and William McKinley damped down their party's social elitism, reversed the Republicans' long-time devotion to soft money, and as a result staked out a vastly increased share of the urban working-class vote in 1896 and thereafter.

This became possible because the very movement that first used the word populist captured the Democratic party, repudiated the hard-money legacy of Jefferson, Jackson, Tilden, and Cleveland, and alienated urban consumers and workers everywhere except in the still largely rural South and West. For the first time in American history, the legacy of economic populism described by Robert Kelley in *The Transatlantic Persuasion* was fairly evenly split between the two parties instead of being mainly the property of the Democrats. This, of course, made it less coherent.

The Progressive movement that erupted in both parties at the turn of the century was profoundly populist in its agenda of political reforms, but it was of more than one mind on economic issues. The split was obvious in the election of 1912, in which Woodrow Wilson took the role of Jefferson to Theodore Roosevelt's Hamilton. As recapitulated in *The Warrior and the Priest* by John Milton Cooper, Jr., Roosevelt believed in large corporations as "indispensable instruments of our modern civilization" whose role was to follow the benign direction of government in directing the wealth they created to the welfare of the common people. Despite his own sunniness, Roosevelt had a somber view of his fellow Americans and often exhorted them to subordinate private interests to the New Nationalism.

Wilson maintained his Jeffersonian optimism about the common people and attacked Roosevelt's economic views as "paternalistic." Following in the footsteps of Adam Smith, he criticized government-business collusion as the source of widespread corruption and called for vigorous enforcement of anti-trust laws. According to Cooper, he "held much more dynamic economic views than Roosevelt. He believed that the main task of reform was to revitalize the economy through governmental actions to open the market to fresh entrants." This put him squarely in the mold of earlier Democratic presidents who fought for cheap land sales and the universal right of business incorporation over strong Federalist and Whig opposition.[4]

Due to the Republican split and economic hard times, Wilson won the election of 1912, but his side of the economic debate was losing in the elite opinion stream to *New Republic* founder Herbert

Croly and his resurrected Hamiltonian elitism. Wilson himself was pulled toward elitism during his first term, just as Democratic presidents would be by a similar trend among liberal elites during the 1960s. The Republicans, meanwhile, regained their hold on the urbanized North, even in their losing presidential race of 1916, and won every industrial state in 1920 and 1924. But they remained at root the party of management and of capital.

The words management and capital sum up an anti-labor, anti-populist mode of thought that gained growing importance in both the public and private sectors. The plausibility of restricting workers to limited, mechanical tasks, endlessly repeated, and carefully supervised by layers of foremen and other managers was inherent in the idea of division of labor from the beginning. Perhaps because of the growing complexity of manufacturing, perhaps also because of the pessimism about people inherited from the pre-egalitarian era, enough early enterprises resembled this model to provide visible targets for a host of critics ranging from Charles Dickens to Karl Marx.

The culmination of elitist management theory was reached by an American mechanical engineer named Frederick W. Taylor. As described by Melvin Kranzberg and Joseph Gies, in Taylor's new discipline, industrial engineering, the role of factory management was "to ascertain the best way to do the job, to provide the correct tools, and to train the worker to act in accordance with precise instructions. Finally, the worker should be provided with an incentive. . . . When each job was rationalized and the worker trained, Taylor timed him with a stopwatch. The worker was then issued an instruction sheet detailing exactly how he was now expected to perform his job, giving the time allotted to each operation, the motions to be employed, the tools to be used. 'What I demand of the worker,' Taylor said, 'is not to produce any longer by his own initiative, but to execute punctiliously the orders given, down to their minutest details.' "[5]

In the years following 1910, Taylorism emerged triumphant in American factories. Those years also saw an upsurge in class conflict and union organizing, widely assumed by businessmen to be a sad but necessary byproduct of industrial efficiency. Only in recent years has a more populist management strategy, of American origin but perfected in Japan, begun to challenge the pessimistic assumptions of Taylorism.

Another blow to the labor theory of value was the rise of capital theory. Adam Smith believed capital was important, but only as a derivative of past labor that made future labor more efficient. But in the nineteenth century economists gave more and more importance to the role of capital as a factor of production that, at least in some sense, preceded labor. The outcome would be to fix most economic creativity in the handful of people and firms who controlled large amounts of capital, rather than in the competence of ordinary people who, in an open economy, could by invention and ingenuity discover new efficiencies of labor.

The exaltation of capital, in some sense a throwback to the mercantilist worship of gold and silver, made strides in the elite opinion stream and created an impression that a regime of popular property rights was one that rewarded the few. Darwinian theory, translated into economics by Herbert Spencer who coined the term "survival of the fittest," added to this impression and was adopted more and more widely by the defenders of property rights no less than its foes. It is symptomatic of the decline of populist economic theory that it was Karl Marx who coined the term "capitalism," but that some of his harshest critics adopted it as their own. Only in recent years has it been argued that small business creates many if not most new jobs in a modern economy, and that even most large corporations seem to start with a handful of workers who attract capital to their idea, rather than by holders of capital having an idea and hiring workers to carry it out.

With the triumph of the New Deal, the economic debate in the United States was almost exclusively among different forms of elitism, as it had long since become in Britain and most of the Continent. The rise of interest-group theory, one of whose assumptions was the need for "protection" of various kinds of workers by various kinds of benign elites, accentuated the irony of later twentieth-century economic politics: never, by any standard, had people scored greater advances in productivity, yet seldom since the coming of mass democracy had the elite opinion stream been more pessimistic about the ability of workers to score such advances on their own.

CHAPTER 3

COMMUNITY STANDARDS

SOCIAL POPULISM is optimism about people's ability to set and observe behavioral standards for their community. Social elitism is optimism about an elite's ability to set and administer standards for a community, or to govern the community without public standards—that is, by discretion.

Any act of government involves either rule by standards or rule by discretion. A community that had neither standards nor discretionary rulers would have no government at all.

In any community, then, two issues concerning standards necessarily precede such seemingly central questions as the goal of government and the identity of the rulers. First, should the community try to operate according to standards or according to the discretion of its rulers? Second, if the choice is to emphasize standards, who will set them—the citizens of the community, or somebody else?

A transition from monarchy to political equality tends to bring with it these answers: it is better for a community to try to operate by standards than by discretion; and it is better for the standards to be set by the citizens of the community, rather than by others, whether these others are native elites or people wholly outside the community.

It is hard to imagine a community wholly without public standards; among other things this would mean a community governed without predictability. Apart from societies ruled by capricious tyrants like Idi Amin, the closest approximation to rule by discretion is in a community ruled by the pure monarchical principle— that is, ownership of the people by the king and/or nobility. In such a society, the ruler has the theoretical right to command without having set standards because his subjects are in some sense his property.

In practice, virtually every government finds it desirable to set standards of some kind. The most dictatorial elite finds it preferable to lay down standards that apply to more than one decision, making it possible for its subjects to comply with its wishes without needing to consult the authorities in each and every case.

At the other extreme, libertarian-minded communities find that standards are necessary to make a decision when freedoms conflict. One person's freedom to smoke a cigar in a public elevator might deny some other person's freedom to breathe smokeless air. The most libertarian community must make a decision on whose freedom takes precedence. This means a decision as to standards, either explicit or tacit, which is political in nature—that is, it applies to every person riding in a public elevator in that community.

So this part of the argument between social populism and social elitism is not so much whether standards are desirable—in almost any conceivable view of politics, at least some are—as over the mix between rule by standards and rule by discretion. An optimistic view of people's social ability would suggest that they are able to understand and live by known rules. The pessimistic view would be that such standards are difficult for people to understand or (due to human passion or selfishness) difficult to observe, requiring a greater role for discretionary decisions by an elite. This is a practical question quite apart from the essentially moral question of what the standards ought to be.

On the other half of the argument—optimism or pessimism about the ability of the people to set the standards they are to observe—the rise of political equality makes social elitism more important, not less. In a climate where it is increasingly difficult to deny people the right to participate in the setting of community standards, pessimism about people's *ability* to do well at this leads to a belief that the people should *delegate* the setting of standards to various elites—elected officials or, more often in recent years, judicial and bureaucratic elites appointed by the elected officials and accountable only tenuously to the people.

In turn, the nature of elite-controlled standard-setting is influenced by the degree of elitism in the other half of the question—the ability of the people to observe known standards. The growth of pessimism in this area would logically lead standard-setting elites to set fewer, more permissive standards, and to demand less accountability on the part of violators. If in the elite opinion stream the belief grows that people or groups of people are incapable of grasping the standards that have been set, it becomes morally suspect to punish violators. This involves a practical issue distinct from the moral question of whether standards should be seen as absolute or relative. A member of a standard-setting elite might believe absolute standards exist, but might still choose not to impose punishment if he believed violators incapable of understanding or observing them.

In democratic countries, a rise in social elitism leads to a de-emphasis of the standard-setting part of political life. Democracy comes to be analyzed as if it involved only the election of leaders, the political "horse race," rather than the setting of community standards. If standard-setting is analyzed at all, it is only as one of the duties of government officials who are mainly involved in discretionary rule. Politics comes to be seen as a competition for power among various elites, who once chosen exercise discretionary rule between elections.

By contrast, classical political theory always started with the setting of standards. The first phrase of Aristotle's *Politics* is, "All human associations are established for some purpose." In *Paideia*, Werner Jaeger describes the struggle for political equality in ancient Greece as largely a struggle for written laws: "Until these struggles began, the right of the nobles to administer justice—

in accordance with traditional usage, not by any written code of laws—had been unchallenged. But as the economic position of the common people improved, the conflict between the freeman of low birth and the nobleman was naturally intensified. Judicial power could easily be misused for political ends. The people demanded written laws. . . . Laws which are written down mean the same for all, high and low alike. After the laws are written, the judges may still be noblemen and not commoners; but they are now bound to administer justice in accordance with the established standards. . . . "[6]

In Athens, the triumph of Solon around 594 B.C. marked the breakthrough to a code of written laws, which was closely associated with his admission of freemen to the assembly. In Rome, a similar process culminated in the publication of the Twelve Tables in 451 B.C., in part modeled on Solon's laws and seen at the time as a victory for the plebs against the patrician-controlled Senate.

In *Concerning Civil Government*, John Locke wrote that the standard-setting, or legislative, function is the "soul that gives form, life, and unity to the commonwealth," and that when the legislative is broken, "dissolution and death follow." Therefore, wrote Locke, "The constitution of the legislative is the first fundamental act of the society, whereby provision is made for the continuation of their union under the direction of persons and bonds of laws made by persons authorized thereunto by the consent and appointment of the people, without which no one man or number of men amongst them can have authority of making laws that shall be binding to the rest." Or, in the words of John Dewey, "The keynote of democracy as a way of life may be expressed as the necessity of the participation of every mature human being in formation of the values that regulate the living of men together." The founders of the United States shared the classical perception almost as a given: "In republican government the legislative authority necessarily predominates" (*Federalist No. 51*).[7]

The contrary view, that the executive is the first order of government, is implicitly monarchical, taking for granted the right of the king or his agents to rule by discretion or to formulate the standards, thus seeing the bulk of the problem in inducing the people to submit to authority—the Hobbesian goal of "order."

That the rise of equality implies a trend from discretion to standards can be seen in the meaning of the word "court." In a ruling monarchy, going to court means visiting the king with a petition and awaiting his judgment by discretion. Each subject has the right to petition the king and therefore, at least potentially, each case is individual. A procedure of this kind still exists in Saudi Arabia.

In civil equality, a court is a forum in which judges and/or randomly appointed citizens (juries) determine which side of an issue is right according to rules known in advance. In the rise of the jury, centuries before the first mass democracies of the West, can be seen the seeds of popular control over standards.

The rise of social elitism is not the only reason for a decline of emphasis on the standard-setting part of politics. There is also a widespread belief in the elite opinion stream that economic motives such as acquisitiveness and class conflict constitute much if not all of the substance of politics.

First, it should be noted that many economic issues can be seen as involving the setting of standards. In most democracies, certain welfare benefits are triggered when the level of one's income falls below a certain standard. The level of taxation varies with the level of income. In each case, a standard must be set before distribution can go forward. The emergence of such institutions as welfare and income taxation are consistent with the trend from monarchical discretion and feudal contracts to egalitarian standard-setting by and for the community as a whole.

Moreover, even in countries such as the United States where economic issues have been prominent, recent research by such historians as Richard Hofstadter, Lee Benson, and Robert Kelley underlines the importance of social issues and of cultural values in determining partisan alignments. In *The Cultural Pattern in American Politics*, Kelley writes, "It has become clear that we can no longer describe the conflict of economic interest groups and assume that the story is complete. Cultural politics is not a side show that occasionally attracts our attention with odd issues like temperance and Sabbatarianism; it is as pervasive and powerful in shaping public life as is the impact of economic politics."[8]

In the United States, this fact was obscured for a time, not only by the school of economic causation founded by Charles Beard, but by the fact that the authors of the Constitution located key economic decisions at the federal level and socio-cultural issues at the state and local level. But battles over community standards often welled up to the national level in cases where states adopted standards which flagrantly contradicted those of the national community, such as Congress's suppression of polygamy in Utah; in cases where an idea broadened its support sufficiently to make an essentially minority movement national, as in the case of both the enactment and the repeal of Prohibition; and above all in the case of slavery, where the national community eventually repudiated the standards of the regional community on an issue which went to the heart of the American commitment to political equality. It is at least arguable that the North would never have come to the brink of war had it not felt threatened by a seeming imposition of regional standards on the nation as a whole, as embodied in the Fugitive Slave Law of 1850 which put federal officials in charge of returning escaped slaves to the South, thus making the legal apparatus of slavery literally visible to many Northerners for the first time.

A more recent issue of community standards, the Supreme Court's 1973 decision taking away the right of the states to curb abortion, was similar to the Fugitive Slave Law in nationalizing an issue previously fought out in the states. At the time that abortion opponents enjoyed a national consensus in the 1950s, when abortion was illegal in virtually all situations in every state, it never occurred to them to take the issue to national forums such as presidential and congressional campaigns. But once an issue becomes nationalized, as abortion was in *Roe v. Wade*, it becomes difficult to confine it to the state and local level, much less to take it wholly out of politics as the Court apparently wished. The intensity of the battle is sharpened by the Court's suppression of legislation and its attempt to remove the issue from democratic debate in a manner widely seen as elitist.

Even before the issue of who chooses the standards, and at what level of government, is the issue of whether a standard is individual or community in nature, and even whether, if it is a community standard, it should attain the force of law. Someone may adopt as an individual standard the performance of a ten-mile run each day, but however valuable this standard may be for him, it is unlikely the community will make it universal. On the other hand, a community might have a universal agreement that being on time to meetings is better than being late, without wanting to apply this standard in binding legislation.

At the other extreme, a community might feel so strongly about a standard that it may want not only to legislate it, but to fix it in a more permanent way. Just as in Greece and Rome the rise of civil equality led to a demand for a written, public code of laws, so the rise of modern equality based on universal human dignity led to a demand for written constitutions, a legal code quasi-permanent in nature—that is, difficult to alter.

Such written constitutions, with their requirements for time-consuming procedures and two-thirds and three-fourths majorities, are often seen as anti-democratic, and as compared to pure democracy perhaps they are. But when standards are easily changeable by a momentary majority, something close to pure discretionary rule can be the result, as many would argue occurred in a number of states under the Articles of Confederation in the 1780s. If standards are easily changeable, one of the standards that can be dropped by an unscrupulous leader is political equality itself, as Hitler proved in the 1930s.

A written constitution is a society's signal of the firmness of its standards. However imperfectly realized, the search for community standards is a search for *fixed* standards, for the more unfixed they are, the less possible it is to regard them as standards at all. Of itself, then, the search for community standards implies social populism—optimism that, acting together, the people can choose appropriate standards, and observe them once they are chosen.

CHAPTER 4

OPTIMISM ABOUT WHAT?

WHY IS POPULISM optimistic about people's ability to make decisions affecting their lives, relative to the ability of elites to make these decisions?

At least in theory, there could be more than one answer, perhaps many possible answers or combinations of answers, depending on the views of various populists on the nature of effective decision-making in people's lives. What kind of decision is it that makes a life good?

For example, a populist who believed that self-interest is the basis of effective decision-making would argue that the people are better at gauging their own self-interest and acting on it than elites, acting on their behalf. A populist who believed that knowledge of a problem is the basis of effective decision-making would argue that only the people have the knowledge of their own lives adequate to make good decisions concerning these lives. A third populist might believe effective decision-making required a combination of the two attributes, knowledge and self-interest, that only the people themselves can lay claim to.

Although any of these hypothetical people would qualify as a populist—someone optimistic about the ability of people to handle their own affairs, relative to the competence of elites—some kinds of populism are evidently more optimistic about people than others, and therefore in some sense more populist than others.

A person, for example, could believe that human beings are predatory by nature, and that therefore a populist-style diffusion of power would make predation less possible and less frequent, when compared with a system concentrating power in an elite. But while perhaps qualifying as populism, this would be one of the least populistic populisms one could imagine, and might better be described as anti-elitism. At the other end of the spectrum would be affirmative versions of populism, for example optimism about people's willingness to undergo personal sacrifice on behalf of a general good. So in general, the degree of populism in any version of populism would seem to depend on interaction with other beliefs about people.

Of particular relevance today is the interaction between populism and political equality, and the emergence of the populist version of equality discussed in Chapter 1—that is, the belief that equality is innate, that it involves dignity rather than value, and that it must therefore be embodied in the present tense of politics.

Such a belief in universal human dignity implies certain things about the *workings* of politics, in particular that citizens should have one vote each and that these votes should be sought and cast on the basis of persuasion, not command. But this vision of equality as universal human dignity would also seem to imply certain things about the nature of the choices made: that inclusion is preferable to exclusion, concord preferable to animosity, cooperation preferable to conflict.

The French revolutionary slogan—Liberty, Equality, Fraternity—best captures this configuration of closely related values. Growth of belief in these three values affects all areas of human life, but in politics it is helpful to see equality as a kind of foundation, at least if the equality embraced is the optimistic vision of universal human dignity in the present tense. Such dignity implies human freedom as an attainable and preferred means of political decision, and fraternity as an attainable and preferred political goal, consistent with present human nature. The belief in fraternity is not a belief that amity universally obtains in the present tense, but that it is a realistic goal of politics, consistent with actual human nature. Someone who believed in equality as humanity's political condition and liberty as its preferred political means, but who believed that fraternity as a serious human goal is excluded by human nature, would be less populist than someone who believed that all three values were attainable.

Some thinkers, both ancient and modern, have believed that fraternity is unattainable, both as an end and as a way of life. Thucydides, Hobbes, Nietzsche, and Herbert Spencer probably fit this category. Very often, such thinkers' rejection of fraternity as a human goal is a natural consequence of their rejection of equality as a human condition, actual or potential.

But in the modern era, which has as its hallmark the acceptance of political equality as either a present fact or future destination, the predominant argument about fraternity has been somewhat similar to the argument about equality: that is, an argument among people who accept fraternity as an important goal of politics, but differ profoundly over how to achieve it.

The names of Kant, Hegel, and Marx are the most prominent in the school that believes that fraternity comes about primarily through conflict. In his essay on *Perpetual Peace*, Kant argues that it is warfare that drives humanity toward unity and concord. Hegel's vision of history ends in synthesis, but only after a protracted clash of ideas. Marx adapted this model to class conflict, which he saw as ending in classlessness and social concord, but only after violent revolution.

At least since Machiavelli, much of Western political theory has given a central role to egoism and conflict as the driving forces of politics. And since the rise of conflict theory coincided with the rise of political equality, populist theory was greatly affected by conflict theory. Locke, Adam Smith, and James Madison come to mind as thinkers populistic in important ways, but pessimistic about people's ability to restrain certain egoistic drives toward acquisition and domination.

The opposing view, which might be called fraternal populism, has fared much better at the level of practice than of theory. It is worth noting that the two most admired political leaders of the nineteenth century in the Anglo-American world, Gladstone and Lincoln, clearly fit into this category. Indeed, the Lincoln-Douglas debates boil down to an argument between fraternal populism and conflict populism, as exemplified by Douglas's doctrine of popular sovereignty, the right of states and territories to enslave or not enslave blacks, depending on a majority vote of whites. As early as 1854, Lincoln attacked the supporters of popular sovereignty for depriving "our republican example of its just influence in the world" by "insisting that there is no right principle of action but *self-interest*" (emphasis in original). Lincoln believed it was no accident that a view which could make domestic human freedom a matter of power politics would also favor the doctrine of imperial expansion known as Manifest Destiny.

Similarly, in an 1862 speech, Gladstone attacked those who argued "that the people cannot be trusted—that they are fit for nothing except to earn daily bread—that you must not call them to the exercise of higher functions, or look to them for enlightened views." As a counter-argument, Gladstone offered the conscious sacrifice of North Country workers who accepted unemployment in the cotton famine triggered by the American Civil War as a necessary share of the fight to end slavery.

If there is one thinker who undermined this kind of fraternal populism in later Anglo-American democracy, it is Charles Darwin. His basic idea—evolution through conflict—was hardly new. Hegel, for one, would have been quick to recognize it, and Darwin himself wrote in *Origin of Species* that he had done no more than apply to biology the economic ideas of Malthus. But the belief that conflict and competition were central not just to human affairs, but to biology itself, gave conflict theory a kind of unassailability, particularly in the elite opinion stream. Only in relatively recent times has a school of biology come to the fore to argue that conflict has been less important than cooperation in explaining biological development.

But in the period when Darwinian conflict theory was on the

rise, it came to permeate Western culture. Not only did it reinforce Marxian class conflict, but it led Marx's fiercest opponents to adopt competition rather than cooperation as the essence of free economic life, via Herbert Spencer's "survival of the fittest." In psychology, Freud, Adler, and Jung agreed, if on little else, that human action was at root egoistic; and Joseph Schumpeter founded modern political science on the premise that democracy was in essence a jungle of elites competing for the affection of a selfish and weak-willed electorate.

In this intellectual atmosphere, it is not surprising that cooperation has gotten short shrift in modern political theory. But the globalizing of Western culture and the growing belief in interdependence may be changing this. Of particular interest is the effect of information technology on people's understanding of social efficacy. In *The Evolution of Cooperation*, Robert Axelrod brings game theory to bear on the question, and concludes that a strategy of cooperation best fits the requirements of most social situations. Historian William H. McNeill, author of *The Rise of the West* and perhaps the most learned modern scholar of comparative culture, concludes, "Conflicting values, of course, exist and mistaken decisions are common. In particular, human life is haunted by persistent tension between long-run and short-run payoffs. But in the aggregate, if relevant statistics could be discovered, they would probably show that long-run payoffs . . . tend to prevail. Such at any rate were the sort of choices enjoined by all the traditional moral codes which civilized mankind inherits. The positive survival value of such codes for individuals and for society at large seems as unquestionable as is the remarkable way in which all the important moral systems of civilized mankind converge in practice toward what Christians know as the Golden Rule."[9]

Far more important than theory has been the visible decline of class conflict as a *fact* in advanced democracy. Switzerland, the most populist of all democracies, has no visible class conflict, and Japan, the most successful and admired of the new post-World War II democracies, has demonstrated that a cooperative social ethic can not only coexist with economic competition, but enhance it.

In a world riven by many visible egoisms and conflicts, the belief in fraternity as anything but a distant goal is far from self-evident. It is perhaps easier to believe in the populist version of equality— universal human dignity as a condition—than to see fraternity as an immediate goal. And even if true that fraternity as a goal is a natural outgrowth of equality as a condition, the spread of full belief in the condition would seem likely to precede widespread acceptance of its consequence or goal.

But a thoroughgoing and consistent egalitarian populism implies something more than slow progress toward fraternity. Just as belief in universal innate dignity implies optimism about people's ability to exercise freedom once given the chance, so it implies optimism about their ability, in a regime of equality and freedom, to attain some measure of fraternity in the present or near present; and fraternity as an immediate goal of political action implies optimism about cooperation rather than conflict as a means of action.

To put it another way, the idea of universal equality dictates inclusion of all people, even those not visible or intimately known, while populism suggests the nature of that inclusion: optimism about the ability of people in the present to make decisions while treating each other with kindness and respect, rather than with aggression and contempt.

Egalitarian elitism tends to agree that political equality, once achieved, implies fraternity as well. But since it sees equality itself as a distant goal, it is not surprising that its pessimism about people in the present extends to pessimism about fraternity. For many egalitarian elitists, especially the Marxists, it is a short step from belief in the unavoidability of egoism and conflict in the present to a welcoming of such conflict as a means toward desired future ends.

Fraternal populism does not deny the importance of political conflict, or rest on some average of human actions in the present. Indeed, a period in which elites believe egoism and conflict to be the keynote of human life can expect to see more aggression and conflict than would otherwise be the case.

Likewise, the major argument is not whether concord, rather

than discord, is a logical goal of human life. Fraternal populism *is* more optimistic than its opponents about the ultimate achievability of a measure of fraternity among people, but its most compelling reason for this optimism is a practical belief that in an age of equality, cooperation can usually outperform conflict as a means of getting there.

CHAPTER 5

ELITES IN HISTORY

THE PRESENCE of elites appears to be universal or nearly universal in civilization. In fact one plausible definition of civilization is a society which generates elites.

The idea of political equality was totally absent from early civilization. Elite rule was universal and taken for granted. Therefore elitism, which as used here is not a synonym for elite rule but a belief system concerning the competence of elites to make decisions on behalf of other people, was non-existent. Any discussion of whether elites were competent to command the people and their resources was academic. Serious disagreements were more likely to concern which elite, or portion of an elite, should command everyone else.

In most of history, then, the idea of political equality never gained a sufficient foothold for arguments between populism and elitism to matter. In a society where the idea of political equality was unknown, in theory the people could overthrow a political elite and establish direct rule. But in practice, elite rule was so taken for granted that the only way for equality to arise was for an elite to be converted to it, or (more frequently) for new elites and types of elites to surface.

Knowledge of the elites that dominated civilization prior to the age of equality is thus helpful not only as a background to elitism, but to an understanding of the origin of political equality itself.

RELIGIOUS ELITES AND BLOOD ELITES

In the entire period from the rise of the first civilizations in Mesopotamia and Egypt around 3000 B.C. until around 600 B.C., elites appear to be based almost exclusively on religious knowledge or on military power. Elites formed out of religious knowledge sometimes, but not always, perpetuated themselves by heredity. Military elites that had staying power invariably became self-perpetuating by heredity. It is difficult to identify a civilized society earlier than 600 B.C. not ruled by blood elites (royalty or nobility), by religious elites, or by some combination of the two.

Cities and civilizations develop when agriculture begins steadily to produce a surplus above subsistence, making possible activity and production that is non-agricultural in nature. In early civilization, most people remained farmers and most production was agricultural; thus the main factor of wealth, for both blood elites and religious elites, was control of the land. Merchants and manufacturers did exist and they could attain considerable wealth when they were permitted a degree of independence from king and priest, but their lack of economic weight compared to agriculture prevented business classes from emerging as important elites until much later in history.

Between 4000 and 3000 B.C., Mesopotamia's emerging cities were ruled mainly by religious elites. The temple bureaucracies of Sumer organized the irrigation that led to steady crop surpluses and were responsible for the development of writing around 3000 B.C. These religious elites gave way to blood elites when the cities' growing wealth began to attract the attention of neighboring barbarians. The first monarchies of the region almost certainly evolved from war leadership.

But religious elites remained important even with the rise of monarchy in the Middle East. Sometimes the two kinds of elites shared power and sometimes they merged, as with the priest-kings of Mesopotamia or the god-kings of Egypt. In the early civilization of the Indus Valley, where warfare was less frequent, religious elites apparently retained sole power until the Aryan conquest around 1500 B.C.

In the later Indian civilization that grew up around the Ganges, warfare remained less important than religion, and therefore so did politics. Monarchy gained the upper hand over primitive democracy as a political system, but religion maintained a separate, independent sphere unknown further west in the Middle East and Egypt. Ironically, one of the major factors that enabled religious life to maintain such power in India was its base in the caste system, itself a form of rule by blood elite.

In the rest of civilization before 600 B.C., religious elites and blood elites were rarely at cross purposes in a single civilization. Sometimes theocracy was established in preference to a more military cast of government, but theocracy was usually a sacerdotal version of monarchy and thus led to succession by inheritance just as in a blood elite of military origin. In non-Indian early civilization, the idea of separation between the governmental sphere and the religious sphere was unknown, except fortuitously when an imperial power proved tolerant of local religious elites following conquest. In pre-Confucian China, separation was unknown because there was no separate religious elite; the blood elite served both as landowner and priest for their households and peasant subjects.

As warfare grew in importance, however, monarchy tended to assume the primary role in its partnership with religion in the major civilizations west of India. At first, military conquest usually meant only that the monarch added to his possessions, lands, and subjects. But beginning with Sargon of Akkad around 2250 B.C., the first recorded imperial conqueror, came the creation of a new form of blood elite: the national or racial elite.

This new elite sometimes took the form of the ownership by members of a conquering nation of members of the subjugated nation, or chattel slavery. In addition, imperial conquest meant permanent alien rule; after a few generations, occupying armies often evolved into imperial bureaucracies. When conquerors failed to develop a lasting empire, a conquering military elite could survive and become a native racial elite, as the Aryans did in India. Soldiers and bureaucrats of long-lived empires like Assyria took on the trappings of an international blood elite.

For most of the period from 3000 B.C. to 600 B.C., or for roughly half of the history of civilization, blood elites and religious elites, often in combination, dominated society by combining possessions, knowledge, and ideas into power over people. This included everything from religious doctrine to crop irrigation and military technology. The power of these elites could not be challenged until new sources of wealth, knowledge, and ideas could grow enough to set up competing claims and power centers.

THE CONFUCIAN KNOWLEDGE ELITE

One kind of alternative to old-line blood and religious elites was found in the teachings of Confucius (551–479) and his disciples, especially Mencius (371–289), between the sixth and second centuries B.C. Confucius challenged the view that nobility was inborn, arguing that it could be attained by study and adoption of a moral code. His belief that the proper destiny of the educated gentleman was to govern, together with Mencius' quasi-egalitarian teaching two centuries later that the justification of the elite's rule was the welfare of the people, introduced a code similar to modern political elitism to the Chinese imperial state.

With the coming to power of the Han dynasty in 202 B.C. in a China newly unified by the militarist Ch'in, Confucianism gradually overcame its opponents, and by 136 B.C. it had put in place a new kind of political elite based not on blood, or military prowess, or religion—the previous dominant elite, the Chou nobles, combined all three—but on education in ideas and knowledge prescribed by the state. This elite was to remain in power until the twentieth century.

At the top, China remained monarchical, and Confucian

bureaucrats worked for the hereditary emperor. But even this was modified by the already ancient teaching on the Mandate of Heaven, the belief that the emperor ruled only so long as he enjoyed the approval of supernatural powers. In contrast to most forms of ruling monarchy, in which the king owned the people as part of his realm, the emperor's uncertain hold on the Mandate of Heaven implied a right of revolution. This too was incorporated into Confucian teaching, and was often invoked by rebels in the declining years of dynasties.

Confucianism was not hostile to religion, but it was hostile to religious elites. Religion in China became a private matter, and as long as it stayed that way it escaped persecution by the state, as Taoism nearly always did. But when a religion showed signs of creating a new power center, as was the case in later centuries with Buddhism and Christianity, the Confucian bureaucracy was more likely to crack down.

A similar situation prevailed with the landowning nobility. Confucian bureaucrats tolerated hereditary control of the land and those who worked it, so long as the nobility remained a mainly economic elite. As centuries passed, many members of the Confucian elite became landowners and many sons of nobles aspired to become Confucian bureaucrats. On balance, the influence of Confucianism made blood much less important in China than in any other long-lived monarchy.

The Confucian elite may have accepted two-thirds of Lincoln's definition of popular rule: government *for* the people (a la Mencius), and government *of* the people (in the sense that those of humble birth could aspire to join the elite). But there was no danger that the third part, government *by* the people, would ever be seen as a logical outgrowth. With its strongly underlined teachings of filial piety and reverence for ancestors, Confucianism was thoroughly hierarchical and conservative. It preserved and stabilized the ultimate authority of the emperor and the political and economic subjugation of most of the people, who were peasants on the land. If Confucianism was a prototype of modern elitism, it was an elitism in a society without a hint of populism.

Confucianism's suspicion of new centers of ideas and power extended to the economic sphere. When in 1430 the Ming emperor outlawed China's vast sea commerce in an attempt to beef up defenses against raiders from the steppes, the efficiency of the Confucian bureaucracy made it possible to enforce the order, with catastrophic results for the future of the empire on the eve of the Age of Exploration. Confucian philosophy denied moral standing to merchants on the grounds that they were parasites. Similarly, it saw the military as at best a necessary evil. In its relative separation from the usual power bases of blood, religion, military power, and personal wealth, the Confucian knowledge elite was unique in the monarchical era of human history. It is not surprising that many *philosophes* of eighteenth-century Europe, advocating a similar break from these alliances, seized on Confucianism as a model.

ECONOMIC ELITES AND ANCIENT DEMOCRACY

Blood elites and religious elites possessed economic power in early civilization, but their economic sway originated in knowledge and power from decidedly non-economic realms. This was true of the Confucians' secular knowledge elite as well.

Just as agricultural surplus created cities and first allowed elites to sustain themselves, broader-based elites had to await economic breakthroughs that made possible not only greater surpluses, but wider distribution of them to economic actors. A third condition was that these new economic actors had to live in or near cities, rather than widely separated from each other. The beginning of political equality thus depended on the rise of urban economic elites.

The first such economic breakthrough was agricultural in nature: the rise of wine and olive oil as unusually profitable export commodities in early Greece, particularly Athens. As described by William H. McNeill in *The Shape of European History*, "In the city's golden age, the citizens of Athens lived modestly, but all had enough to eat without working very hard. Vineyards and olive groves of the modest size ordinary Athenians possessed required some 60 to 80 days' work per annum; the rest of the time men could devote safely enough to noneconomic concerns. Indeed, the real measure of the city's wealth was the leisure its citizens enjoyed without starving."[10]

Also important in classical Greece was a change in military technology: the decline in dominance of the cavalry, which had favored landed aristocracies because of the expense of maintaining horses, and the rise of a closely drilled infantry formation, the phalanx. The creation of a broader-based military elite made possible the rise of the distinctive Greek city-state, the *polis*, even before the rise of radical democracy in Athens and elsewhere. Later, when the Athenian navy became important, the precedent of awarding citizenship to a pivotal new military elite was extended to rowers.

As mentioned in Chapter 3, Solon around 594 B.C. took a major step toward civil equality by giving Athens a set of written laws. One of those outlawed the practice of debt-slavery. Solon also forgave outstanding debts, restoring many small farmers to their land and to relative social equality. Around 560 B.C. the tyrant Peisistratus gave the dawning oil and wine industry broad-based economic stimulus by granting low-interest loans to farmers who converted their land to grapes and olives (which takes several barren years to accomplish).

Athenian culture in the sixth and fifth centuries B.C. also involved new political ideas, as well as improvements in military technology. But the breakthrough to a new form of civilization would nevertheless have been unlikely without the rise of the new economic elites, according to McNeill: "The special quality of Athenian culture in its Golden Age, when custom lost its hold and everything had to be examined and considered afresh, was deeply tinctured by this unique geo-economic balance between an oil-wine export metropolis and a hinterland eager to accept all that the Athenians and their fellow Greeks cared to spare from their own consumption of these commodities. In particular, the equal participation of citizen farmers in the affairs of the Athenian polis was sustained by the active role these same farmers had in the production and marketing of the wine and oil whose export, more than anything else, sustained the entire Athenian economy. City folk could not afford to scorn and deride those whose land and labor provided such a vital link in the city's prosperity; still less could they neglect the armed and organized might of these same stalwart farmers, concentrated in the city's phalanx. . . . The Athenian farmers were free men, each the master of himself and his land, head of his family and household, and an autonomous participant in public affairs, with the right to vote on all important matters of policy."[11]

Contemporary Greeks such as the historian Herodotus attributed Athens' pre-eminence to this unleashing of human energy: "Thus did the Athenians increase in strength. And it is plain enough . . . that freedom is an excellent thing; since even the Athenians who, while they continued under the rule of tyrants, were not a whit more valiant than any of their neighbors, no sooner shook off the yoke than they become decidedly the first of all. These things show that, while undergoing oppression, they let themselves be beaten, since they worked for a master; but so soon as they got their freedom, each man was eager to do the best he could for himself."[12]

Athens was no modern democracy. Women, slaves, aliens, and other non-citizens constituted perhaps 90 percent of the city's population, and non-Greeks were slaves "by nature," according to Aristotle. When he and others wrote about equality, they usually meant a rough equivalence of social condition.

The raw power such social equality unleashed was, moreover, gradually channeled to imperialism, which gave the Athenian citizenry the look of a national blood elite, at least in the eyes of its victims among the other city-states. When the chief route to citizenship passed from oil and wine exporting to rowing for the imperial navy, the interdependence between democracy and conquest became obvious, and it gave Athenian democracy a bad name.

The rise to power of an economic elite that attained a measure of social and political equality nevertheless provided a laboratory that inspired contemporary and later thinkers. It created a vocabulary facilitating talk about such things as the people and aristocracy, democracy and oligarchy, tyranny and freedom. Because social equality led first to a form of civil equality in 594 B.C., and then to a form of political equality with the overthrow of the Peisistratid tyranny in 510 B.C., the political debate involved arguments very similar to the modern one between populism and elitism, as in Herotodus' assertion of the military superiority of democracy to monarchy in enabling Athens to defeat the Persian Empire.

Across the Adriatic, the early rise of the Roman republic had a surprisingly similar economic base—in a wine and oil export boom; and the publication of a code of written laws, the Twelve Tables in 451 B.C., laid the basis for civil equality similar to Solon's in Athens a century and a half earlier. But, compared to Athens, a weighted voting system based on tribal membership strongly modified Roman political equality, and the rise of the Senate, a self-perpetuating blood elite that had particularly important sway in foreign and military policy, gradually eroded the role of the electorate long before the fall of the republic. Like Athens, Rome saw many political struggles that had a populist-elitist cast, most noticeably in the period of the land distributions of the Gracchae. More often, Roman politics seemed a self-serving struggle among classes and elites, rather than a struggle of ideas.

Among those who wrote about ancient democracy at the time, Herodotus was an exception in favoring it. On the other hand, Thucydides, the Athenian general who chronicled the defeat of Athens by Sparta in the Peloponnesian War, blamed it on Athenian democracy. When forced to explain the democracy's early victories under Pericles, Thucydides employed an argument often to be repeated by critics of democracy: because of Pericles' brilliance, Athens during his years was a democracy only "in name."

Perhaps the greatest contradiction in ancient democracy was its attitude to the nature of political equality, particularly when applied to those beyond the scope of citizenship, such as slaves and opponents in war. The rise of economic and military elites to citizenship elevated politics to a new framework, broader-based than was possible under blood and religious elites of the past. The multiplication of leisured elites could lead to civil equality, to de-mocracy, and to arguments that resembled those between populism and elitism. But as long as numerically significant elites were restricted to wealthy cities and their surrounding vineyards and olive groves, the possibility of equality beyond the city limits was far from self-evident. In the ancient world, and in the world of many centuries to come, the vast majority of people was tied to the land producing less profitable crops, controlled by numerically small blood elites who deployed them and their resources virtually at will. A rich egalitarian city-state like Athens or Rome was more likely to see these foreign peasantries as targets of conquest than as candi-dates for equality.

Aristotle's pupil Alexander the Great tried to replace the polis with the cosmopolis, a world state in which Greek and barbarian had equal dignity. But by then Greek democracy was dead as a military power and the successor Hellenistic culture was becoming as completely monarchical as any civilization of the ancient Middle East. Similarly, by the time Cicero enunciated the Stoic teaching of universal human dignity in a world-state, he was doing so in the first century B.C., in a Roman republic that was on the verge of becoming a full-fledged monarchy.

The Greeks and Romans were more important as experimenters in political equality than as definers of it. By the time their experi-ences in urban equality had led some of their thinkers in the direction of universal equality, the experiment was either over or no longer influential.

The idea of equality in the modern sense of natural human dignity became more widely understood with the spread of univer-sal religions, particularly Christianity, Islam, and Mahayana Bud-dhism. But universal religions dealt in ultimate issues, and in return for freedom in their own realms they were often willing to cede monarchs a degree of legitimacy in theirs.

More important, the idea of universal equality is closely bound up with the unity of all people, as it clearly was in the mind of Alexander. As long as democracy could not be imagined in anything larger than a city-state, the idea of universal human dignity was more likely to lead to visions of universal empire or a world-state—a monarchy almost by definition—than to advocacy of equal political rights for all people.

In a world dominated by monarchy, efforts to establish or maintain democracy were far more likely to be posed in terms of rights and liberties, many of them assertedly ancient, than on grounds of human equality that made too dangerously direct a challenge to monarchy. This is indeed what happened in the Europe of the Middle Ages, as Quentin Skinner documents in the early pages of his classic, *The Foundations of Modern Political Thought.* The full implications of equality for politics would have to wait for cultural, economic, and technological developments of a much later time.

MULTIPLICATION OF MODERN ELITES

The new political elites of ancient Athens and Rome had their origin of power in agriculture, though later military developments cemented this power. Small-plot olive and grape farming provided the only combination of numbers, leisure, and closeness to the city that could have led to ancient democracy. When olive and grape farming spread to other parts of the Mediterranean and thus declined sharply in profitability, political equality was already in being and could be maintained for a time on other bases of power, political and military.

But there were clear upper limits on how far expansion of an electorate could go on a purely agricultural basis. The large-acreage grain farming that dominated the ancient world and most of the history of civilization could give rise to a wealthy elite with leisure. But its small numbers and distance from each other made it unlikely that such an elite could evolve from a nobility to an electorate, or even a significant part of an electorate.

Moreover, since citizen-owned olive groves and grape orchards could be (and usually were) passed from father to son, new agricultural elites were never far from becoming old-style blood elites. As ancient city-state democracies grew in wealth, they either tended to become divided between citizens and have-nots, or they tried to retain a broad-based citizenry by enfranchisement of soldiers and sailors, as happened in both Athens and Rome. This went hand-in-hand with the transformation of the citizenry into an international blood elite under imperialism.

The rise of new agricultural elites caused the birth of political equality. But the very potency associated with ancient political equality, together with the limits on agriculturally based electorates, led these mass-based agricultural elites to evolve into quasi-military elites, and thus to an imperialism that proved incompatible with democracy itself.

It was, of course, possible to maintain democracies without either new elites or cities. This was done for centuries in what is now eastern Switzerland by means of *Landesgemeinden*, mass assemblies of the male citizenry that met annually to make laws and elect members of the executive and judicial branches. Here the social equality was ancient, perhaps pre-civilizational, and the problems of proximity were overcome by having infrequent meetings.

But however important as a stimulus to such later thinkers as Rousseau, the democracy of the Swiss mountains could not provide a direct spur to democratization in a civilized world divided mainly between grain agriculture and cities. The Swiss herders were part of neither world, and their way of life could not be implanted beyond their highly defensible mountains. A democracy maintained with few if any elites, moreover, does not generate native political theorists who draw lessons from its experience and spread them abroad. The success of the Swiss in remaining independent of the Habsburg and other covetous monarchies excited much admiration in Europe (not to mention a demand for Swiss mercenaries), but imitation of these direct democracies in societies that were both more complex and less compact proved an unlikely line of advance for democratic experimentation.

In a world dominated by blood elites and a peasant majority, several things had to happen for political equality to gain wider application. First, rising economic elites would have to include greater numbers of people than seemed possible if the elites were purely agricultural. Second, these elites had to find a way to extend the influence of their way of life beyond the cities and into the countryside, which contained the bulk of the people. Finally, these economic elites would have to gain independent political power; that is, power not dependent on their transformation into elites of a more traditional sort that inevitably meant the reassertion of inequality.

One or even two of these conditions could be accomplished for a time, and with powerful effects; but all three had to coincide for an extended period for the dominance of monarchy to give way to some form of political equality in an extensive territorial state.

The rise of the first commercial civilization in China starting around A.D. 1000 fulfilled the first two conditions, but not the third. A way of life based on voluntary exchange rather than coercion spread from Chinese cities into the countryside, especially when farmers gained the right to pay taxes by money rather than by an elite exaction of crops. The invention of paper money made surplus wealth easily fungible and contributed to an explosion of market activity and culture.

But as mentioned earlier, the Confucian elite retained its political monopoly under the emperor, and the suppression of sea voyaging underlined how unquestioned that monopoly was. Like the aristocratic landowners before them, merchants and manufacturers in medieval China put the highest value not on building lasting enterprises, but on making enough money to permit their leisured sons to study for the Confucian bureaucracy. For all their dazzling originality, the makers of the first broad-based commercial civilization never gained serious political leverage of their own.

Ironically, one of the central reasons for the emergence of Chinese commercial civilization—the vast extent and political stability of the empire—was also a central reason why new economic elites, numerous as they were, could not rise to political power. Ultimately, the emperors and the Confucian knowledge elite were able to keep their vast domain centralized, leaving no islands of independence where new economic elites could learn to exercise political skills.

The commercial elites that later arose in Europe were luckier. They benefited from Europe's chronic political division. Indeed, the city-states of northern Italy defined their republican beliefs not in terms of political equality but as a way of maintaining independence from the universalist claims of the Holy Roman Empire.

The medieval city-states of Europe rarely forwarded an alternative universalism of their own, but to survive and grow they didn't need to. Because no one monarchy could dominate, capitalists found ways of playing off one king against another, and economic growth took on an independent dynamic of its own. Not only were maritime economic states like Venice and Genoa able to develop far-flung outposts and interests while maintaining republican institutions at home, but new economic classes and professions were gaining a kind of international independence. Banking families like the Fuggers of Augsburg, whose interests lay beyond the control of any one sovereign, became as influential in making war possible as were the blood elites of the territorial monarchies.

The world of international money multiplied itself and gave birth to new elites—artistic, scientific, and educational—as well as new economic ones. Even when territorial monarchies began to absorb the city-states of Italy and Germany, new ideas and elites were too powerful and attractive for monarchy to destroy, or want to destroy. If Charles V had been able to do in Europe what the Chinese emperors or the Japanese shoguns had done in Asia, the story might have been different. As it was, according to William H. McNeill in *The Rise of the West*, the rise and staying power of new elites gave Europe by 1600 a complex, multinational, cosmopolitan texture that permitted active participation by a far larger proportion of its population than in any other part of the earth.

Almost from the beginning, commercial elites in the city-states won the allegiance of neighboring territories, as the German historian Otto of Freising noted in a visit to Italy in the middle of the twelfth century. He noticed that "practically the entire land is divided among the cities" and that "scarcely any noble or great man can be found in all the surrounding territory who does not acknowledge the authority of his city."[13]

Thus alliances of commercial city-states, replete with their economic growth and constant generation of new elites, had the possibility of gaining territorial sovereignty with a citizenry of unprecedented size. But in Italy, such coalitions constantly formed and reformed, and most city-states (with the notable exception of Venice) passed to rule by blood elites by the sixteenth century. In Northern Europe, the Hanseatic League had great economic leverage but little political unity among its squabbling component states.

The right conditions for a territorial regime of equality were finally generated by the cauldron of the Dutch revolt (1568–1609). These included the rise of Calvinism, the need for unity against the powerful Spanish monarchy of Philip II, and a predominantly commercial explosion that included significant manufacturing and agricultural elements. The elites that were able to bring into being the Dutch Republic had little in common and often feuded, and their state was republican mainly in theory. But for the first time a significant land area committed to political equality impressed the world of monarchy by its economic and cultural power and by its global military reach.

The Dutch Republic had an agricultural component more extensive than could obtain in any one city-state, but much of its urban political base was a leftover of medieval privilege, and its economic power was mainly in its status as a financial center. Moreover, essential as the multiplication of new elites was to the *possibility* of political equality, it was no guarantee.

As so often in the past, the protean institution of monarchy adapted to the challenge. Not only were many of Europe's republican city-states absorbed, but such monarchs as Louis XIV made the new elites centerpieces of a cultural renaissance. In the later seventeenth century, war with France drained the Dutch Republic of men and resources, relegating it to second-class status as a power. This could always happen as long as the territorial monarchies controlled the bulk of the population and could accept and assimilate the new sources of wealth.

In larger countries, most of the people were on the land. A corner of civilization could be dominated by new urban elites, but such corners were always vulnerable to the agricultural-based manpower of territorial empires and monarchies. The rise of economic elites and pluralism in the cities was essential, but until a measure of broad-based equality could establish itself in a large nation—which meant one with a majority of farmers—the new elites could not overthrow the blood and religious elites that still dominated the bulk of humanity as recently as the seventeenth century.

THE ENGLISH GENTRY

That the breakthrough toward the curbing of territorial monarchy came in seventeenth-century England has been attributed to innumerable factors, some of which England shared with more limited gains achieved earlier by commercial city-states and the Dutch Republic. These included the growth of commerce and the rise of new urban elites; the sixteenth-century gains of Calvinism and the growing tendency of religious allegiance to outweigh allegiance to a given monarch when these two were in conflict; and the related willingness of political thinkers such as the Scottish philosopher George Buchanan to assert a right of popular revolution against monarchs who were judged to have breached ancient contracts with the people.

If there was a significant difference between England and the Continent it was in the rise of a broad-based rural elite, the gentry, that was able to translate its economic gains into national political power. It did this through revival of an ancient institution that had fallen into disuse, the Parliament.

The spread of commercial methods to English farms was important, as was the gentry's windfall from the confiscation of the monasteries by Henry VIII. But these developments had parallels on the Continent.

The one economic factor almost unique to England in the sixteenth century was the growing trend toward enclosure, the displacement of peasants from age-old possession of common lands and their conversion into private property. The increasing profitability of the woolen trade gave the gentry a broader economic base as enclosure spread. Ironically, the displacement of the rural poor by the gentry was a key factor in leading to the first broad-based rural elite in a territorial monarchy, which in turn decisively ended the age-old assumption that representative institutions could take root only in cities.

The vehicle for these gains was Parliament, particularly the House of Commons. Relatively powerless under the authoritarian Tudor monarchy, in the early seventeenth century Parliament emerged as a growing rival to King James I, the first of the Stuart dynasty to rule in England as well as in Scotland. "To a remarkable degree," writes R. K. Webb, "the ambitions of the gentry had come to center on Parliament: as natural leaders of their communities, they felt they belonged there; it sat at Westminster, where the fashionable world also assembled, and good behavior there might earn favorable notice and open possibilities of office. Peers, the titled aristocrats, sat in the House of Lords as a matter of right. But their sons, who were commoners at law (unlike Continental aristocracies), and the heads of prominent gentry families sought election to the Commons. They gradually took over the representation of England's towns, which counted far more seats than the counties for which sons of peers or leading gentry might naturally stand. . . . The Crown was under constant pressure to increase the number of seats, and from 298 members in the first Parliament of Henry VIII the membership rose to 467 in the first Parliament of James I."[14]

Religious controversies, foreign policy, and taxation were crucial factors in the mounting estrangement between the Stuart kings and Parliament. But in a world where monarchs were assumed to control the people and their output as a matter of right, a legal basis was needed for Parliament to challenge the crown on these and other issues. Much of this was provided by still another rising elite: lawyers.

First as a chief justice of the Court of Common Pleas and later as a member of the House of Commons, Sir Edward Coke was the central figure in elaborating the idea that the common law, an unbreakable "fundamental law" of the people, took precedence over what the king *or* Parliament could enact. By 1628, Parliament in the Petition of Right declared it illegal for the king to collect money without parliamentary consent. Coke and his allies claimed ancient precedent was on their side, but their assertion of popular community standards and control of the purse was something very new in an extensive territorial state.

How big was the rural electorate that backed up these claims? An adult free male could vote if he held land earning 40 shillings a year. This represented a small minority in a rural England still struggling to emerge from feudalism. But in the overseas colonies in North America, where land was plentiful and feudalism never existed, the same requirement meant that as many as 75 percent of adult freemen could vote for legislator, and in two colonies even for governor. This meant a mass-based and yet predominantly rural electorate—a first in human history. The implications were (and proved to be) revolutionary.

The English Parliament dated back to folkmoots, Anglo-Saxon tribal assemblies whose origins, like the similar *Landesgemeinden* of the Swiss mountains, lay in the mists of prehistory—that is, before the rise of civilization and its elites. Civilization meant organized agriculture and agricultural surplus, which always went hand in hand with elite control of the bulk of the people, who were small farmers. The English gentry became the first elite to stake a powerful and lasting claim to represent (rather than simply direct) a majority farming population, using this pre-civilizational leftover. By claiming a kind of ultimate sovereignty for an assembly that predated anything approaching civilized monarchy, the gentry was laying the basis for political revolution and for the destruction of monarchy. It was a member of the gentry, Oliver Cromwell, who ordered the execution of Charles I in 1649.

The establishment of a regime of political equality under the Commonwealth was a traumatic event for most English elites. Cromwell himself dismissed Parliament and exercised monarchical powers as Lord Protector. The monarchy was restored in 1660 without a fight, and even after Parliament regained the political upper hand in the Glorious Revolution of 1688, English political life retained a monarchical vocabulary. This meant, among other things, a downplaying of the implications of universal equality. Like the independent city-states which lived in the shadow of powerful emperors and kings in the medieval period, English reformers preferred to speak of liberties and rights, preferably as ancient as possible, rather than innate equality, in their steady efforts to chip away the power of the blood elites.

Except for the Interregnum (1649–60), England's commitment to equality was implicit rather than explicit. Something about political equality seems to make it difficult to enshrine until the monarch is explicitly removed—in North America by a colonial revolt, in France by regicide and revolution. England pioneered some of the seminal institutions of the age of equality—the independent legislature, the political party, and cabinet government, to name a few—but it was left to the post-monarchical regimes of North America and France to evangelize equality in the nineteenth century, and it was not until after the period 1911–22—when, in quick succession, the ruling monarchies of China, Russia, Austria-Hungary, Germany, and Turkey came crashing to the ground—that the age of equality began in earnest for mankind as a whole.

CHAPTER 6

ELITES AND ELITISM

JUST AS ELITES inaugurated the age of equality, the age of equality brought forth elitism. This was a natural step, given the nature of monarchy and of equality.

The world of monarchy was a world of command. The physical power base was military skill and inherited land, which included the people on it. Political and religious ideas were a factor in sustaining monarchy. These included the divine right of kings and the Confucian belief that the highest life for a gentleman was to participate in the imperial bureaucracy. But the essence of government was to establish standards and exercise discretion over the people and over things; in short, to command.

Today's world of presently recognized political equality, or democracy, is a world of persuasion. Ideas, knowledge, and arguments therefore rise in relative importance. Command exists, but by consent of the community. Consent by definition takes prior persuasion.

Persuasion could be an important factor in the world of monarchy, as in the Confucians' successful sixty-six-year effort (202–136 B.C.) to persuade the Han Dynasty to install their philosophy as the Chinese Empire's official belief system. Five centuries later, persuasion of a single monarch made Christianity the official religion of the Roman Empire.

But when political equality is recognized in the present, the people are acknowledged as sovereign, and persuasion becomes an even greater factor because consent is needed from so many more people.

Money is an important tool of mass persuasion. So are ideas, expertise, and eloquence. The rise of elites possessing these tools was an important factor in undermining the legitimacy of monarchy, and such elites become instantly and visibly more important as soon as regimes of equality are established.

As such new elites appear and grow in membership and importance, achievement tends to supplant blood as a mark of elite status. One reason the growth of elites threatened late monarchy is that a larger and larger share of those belonging to elites had gotten there by economic, intellectual, and other forms of achievement, rather than by being someone's son or daughter. As the complexity of society grew, the moral basis for rule by blood elite was gradually undermined.

Once equality was established, partially as in England or explicitly as in the United States and France, achievement elites grew even faster. Blood elites survived, and even occasionally regained power, as in Restoration France (1815–30), but in the world of persuasion a mere assertion of an innate right to rule seemed more and more inadequate. Increasingly, blood elites related their fitness to rule to criteria involving merit and achievement (attendance at the right schools, traditions of *noblesse oblige*, etc.).

Moreover, even if a blood elite could retain ultimate control in a society with rapidly multiplying elites, as in nineteenth-century Germany, the number of new realms of attractive activity meant new realms for elite sway. And once egalitarian ideas began to advance in such a complex society, as they inevitably did, elites felt called upon to justify their importance in the nation at large, as well as in their own growing realms—business, educational, legal, journalistic, and all the rest. This often, though by no means always, involved elitist argumentation.

Sir Robert Walpole, the Whig prime minister of England (1721–42), was a member of the gentry but maintained and expanded his power by policies of peace and prosperity and by constructing through patronage the first modern party elite. The rise of such figures gave encouragement not only to other politicians but to rising elites in non-political areas of life. People who had entered an elite by achievement were often committed to equality of opportunity. They believed that having an impact on the lives of other people had to be earned, through work and knowledge. But having achieved elite status through work and knowledge, it is not surprising that some of them believed they could make superior decisions for those they had left behind. This is elitism.

Elitists should not be seen as closet royalists, or as necessarily less than wholehearted in their belief in equality. The belief in human equality, in the sense of present, innate equality as stated in the Declaration of Independence or the Declaration of the Rights of Man, is a moral statement. The argument between populism and elitism is an argument about the relative competence of people and elites, and is practical in character.

As noted earlier, monarchy is unlikely to give way to democracy unless a substantial portion of the elite opinion stream becomes egalitarian, or populist, or both. Alexander Hamilton was a member of the American elite who was also elitist in the context of American politics. This did not stop him from being an eloquent advocate of representative government in the *Federalist Papers*. George Washington was also elitist in belief, but that did not prevent him from risking his life and fortune for political equality and repeatedly condemning the idea of an American monarchy with himself as king.

Other key members of the American elite of the late eighteenth century were egalitarian *and* populist, and formed the Democratic-Republican party in the 1790s to fight the more elitist Federalists led by Washington, Hamilton, and John Adams. The presidential victories of Thomas Jefferson and James Madison in the early nineteenth century laid the groundwork for a populist interpretation of American equality. The optimism of such leaders undoubtedly sped the virtually universal enfranchisement of white males that perhaps would have happened anyway. But the enlargement of the franchise did not end the argument between populism and elitism in the United States, nor has it done so in any other country.

KNOWLEDGE ELITES VS. MONEY ELITES

In the democratic world of fully realized political equality, elitism almost by its nature involves the claim to superior knowledge.* The gaining of wealth may give a person elite economic status, and it could enable him to increase his political influence either legally (a campaign contribution) or illegally (a bribe). But elitism is not the same thing as elite status or elite influence. Elitism is the belief that the elite in question can make superior decisions on behalf of others, and when these others have an equal political say, they are likely to cede their right to make decisions only to those who make a strong case for their possession of greater relevant knowledge.

In money elitism, this claim to superior knowledge is in fact present. Alexander Hamilton, the founder of American money elitism, argued that political and banking elites knew better where the nation's investments should go—namely, to the creation of new manufacturing industries. Later, capital theory came forward not as a statement that capitalists should rule because they have more money, but that large holders of capital were more likely to make good economic decisions than were workers or small property holders.

Yet despite its reliance on knowledge, money elitism is a form of knowledge elitism so important in democracy that it can be seen as a

* The other human mental faculty, will, has often been cited as a claim to superiority. But the assertion that the will power of a group or elite is qualitatively superior is so stark that it generally goes beyond mere elitism into a belief in outright inequality. This was true of defenders of slavery in the United States and of later believers in a "master race" in Germany and elsewhere.

separate form of elitism. Money elites, moreover, often seem to be in conflict with "pure" knowledge elites. In *The Age of Reform*, Richard Hofstadter argues that the broad-based, democratizing Progressive movement that gained dominance in both parties around the turn of the century could be seen as a counter-attack against new corporate elites by knowledge elites such as lawyers, clergy, and journalists, who had lost the social and political pre-eminence Tocqueville had observed in the United States in the first half of the nineteenth century.

Antagonism between these two major types of achievement elites—money elites and knowledge elites—appears to increase as political equality is achieved, though the conflict is by no means inevitable.

Money elites and knowledge elites, on the other hand, are most likely to be allied in fights against political inequality. In the North's fight against American slavery, money elites and knowledge elites (in particular, the clergy) were among the most militant against the South. While the pattern was not so clear-cut in Gladstone's unsuccessful battle for Irish Home Rule in the 1880s and 1890s, knowledge elites and money elites were far more likely to take the Liberal side of the argument than were blood elites and the *established* (Church of England) religious elites, who were almost unanimously opposed.

This is not surprising. Achievement elites were instrumental in establishing democracy, and once it is established they benefit far more from social and political equality than do blood elites. In political fights to preserve or enhance equality, they are naturally drawn to alliance against elites who would center status on blood rather than achievement. It is in an atmosphere of more fully achieved political equality, or in a period that does not so directly involve issues of political equality as did the battles against Southern slavery and in favor of Irish Home Rule, that the chronic antagonism between money elites and knowledge elites is likely to arise.

This has a direct impact on the nature of populism at any given time in history. In the United States as the nineteenth century wore on, and especially after the Republicans instituted elitist, pro-industrial policies in the 1860s and after, populism's chief target was money elitism, particularly the kind centered in banking and manufacturing. First the Mugwumps, then the Populists, and finally the Progressives, waged war on behalf of the direct party primary, direct election of senators, and initiative, referendum, and recall in a more and more radical effort to break up the alliance between large, multi-state corporations and political parties, particularly the Republicans. Throughout the nineteenth century, from Jefferson, Jackson, and Van Buren, all the way to Tilden, Cleveland, Bryan, and even Wilson, populism was anti-business in theme and heavily economic in content. This was true for heirs of the Jeffersonian tradition, Cleveland and Bryan, who loathed each other in every other way. Cleveland's attacks on big-business bribery and tariff-raising were interchangeable with Bryan's attacks on big-city banks and corporations, except that Bryan was attacking them as authors of deflation.

The Progressive movement enacted its agenda of populist political reforms, shattering the hold of corporate elites on many governments at the state and local level. But the alliance between corporate America and the Republican party remained firm in presidential politics, and it took the Depression and the New Deal to eject corporations from the central power position of American political life.

Understandably enough, the New Deal's intellectual backbone was made up of rising knowledge elites, including academics, social activists, and lawyers. Part of the premium on knowledge rather than money related to the nature of New Deal-favored economic and social planning, which presumed superior knowledge of economic and social reality on the part of the planning elites. But the pattern of conflict between knowledge elites and money elites in the 1930s and 1940s was hardly unique to that period, and may be a natural tendency in a democracy where political equality is either fully achieved, or not a paramount issue at the time in question.

Knowledge elites were important from the Revolution on in the United States, but the New Deal marked the first time knowledge elitism attained national power and prominence. After 1932, old-fashioned anti-business populism did not disappear any more than did business elitism, but because of the greater prominence of knowledge elitism in the New Deal cycle, the populist impulse inevitably took on a more anti-government and at times anti-intellectual contour than it had before.

THE ELITE OPINION STREAM

Two dictionary definitions of elite point up two different kinds of elite: "The choice or select part; esp., a group or body treated as socially superior" (*Webster's*, 1961); "the best or most skilled members of a given social group" (*American Heritage*, 1973).

Lawyers are (and were from the beginning) an elite group in American democracy. A judge, or a president of a state bar association, or a professor of law, would qualify as an elite member within this elite group.

Steelworkers are not (and never have been) an elite group in American democracy. The president of the steelworkers union is an elite member of this non-elite group.

Steelworkers as steelworkers are members of the popular opinion stream. Only by some specific elite achievement would a steelworker become a member of the elite opinion stream. A steelworker could become an officer in his union, or he could also attain elite status by becoming chairman of a major political party in his county or by obtaining a PhD.

Lawyers as lawyers are members of the elite opinion stream, in part because they hold an advanced degree, still by and large a mark of elite status in the United States. But that lawyers are members of the elite opinion stream says nothing about whether a given lawyer holds populist or elitist views, or even whether lawyers as a whole (at any given time) are more or less elitist than is public opinion as a whole.

Membership in some other groups in society is not so clear-cut, in terms of its conferring (or not conferring) of elite status. In business, to take one such example, few would deny elite status to the chairman of General Motors, and few would confer it on the manager of the local convenience store. Yet both are businessmen. The gradations in between are countless, and could be the source of endless disagreement.

Definitions of the elite opinion stream, then, could differ widely. Yet on reflection few would disagree that in any given community, some people have elite status while others do not. This being so, there is such a thing as an elite opinion stream and a popular opinion stream, which are distinct from each other, however hard they are to define and regardless of what views prevail in each opinion stream at any given time.

Vice President Walter Mondale recognized this distinction in a 1980 interview with political analyst Alan Baron. Asked about Democratic election defeats in 1978, Mondale said: "In looking at this I often recall something John Gardner told me. He told me that his faith in the future was maintained by his conviction that, throughout America, there was a community of thinking, caring people who read books and thought about the future of the country. These are the people we have to reach."[15] Although Mondale said nothing about this group's beliefs, and would have been hard pressed to sum them up if he had tried, he is clear about the existence of an influential opinion stream that can be distinguished, and appealed to in different ways, from the overall group of voters who had produced his party's election defeats. Though their terminology might differ widely, most political leaders are well aware of this distinction and tailor their appeals to each opinion stream accordingly.

It is possible for the elite opinion stream to be more populist than the popular opinion stream; that is, at a given time the elites in a community may be more optimistic about the people's ability to handle their own problems than are the people themselves. This may very well have been the case in France prior to the Revolution, when egalitarian and populist ideas swept much of the elite opinion stream including elements of the nobility and royal family, while much of the predominantly rural population retained monarchist assumptions.

But in an already established democracy, such an alignment between the popular and elite opinion streams, while perhaps not unthinkable, would be unusual. In a regime of political equality, the elite opinion stream has a natural tendency toward elitism, the belief that elites tend to make better decisions on behalf of people than do the people themselves. Elitism might or might not hold a majority within the elite opinion stream, but it would be surprising if it did not command a higher proportion among elites than it did among members of the popular opinion stream.

If the elite opinion stream provides a natural base for elitism, not to mention a virtual monopoly of *articulate* elitism, it stands to reason that the more complex a society, the more elitism it will tend to have. Even clearer, since a complex society means a society with many kinds of elites, such a society will contain more kinds of elitism than will a society with relatively few elites, such as Athens in the fifth century B.C. or even the United States of the early nineteenth century.

One kind of elitism, of course, may totally disagree with another, particularly in an area where the elites in question have a natural conflict. Business elitism is very different from union elitism; however much the two kinds of elitism might agree on their pessimism about the members of the labor force, they would strongly disagree as to which elite's decision-making ability they are optimistic about.

It is, nevertheless, natural that the elites in a complex society should interact with and influence each other, particularly in their areas of expertise. A journalistic elite may disagree on most issues with business elites while tending to defer to them on issues relating to business investment.

An example of this can be found in a *Washington Post* editorial of April 15, 1983, which stated that "manipulation of the tax code isn't a terribly effective way of changing most people's habits in managing their personal money. It works beautifully in the business sector, where funds are handled by professionals using the tax system's incentives to increase returns. But people very frequently have other values to follow in disposing of their own incomes." This statement of the relative effectiveness of tax cuts for business as compared to tax cuts for individuals is a standard belief of American (and other) business elites. That it does not appear to be borne out by recent experiences in high-growth Japan (which has low personal taxes and high business taxes) and in low-growth Western Europe (high personal taxes and low business taxes) is beside the point. The tendency of one segment of the elite opinion stream is to accept the expertise of some other elite, if only in that one area of putatively superior knowledge. The tendency to elitism in those who have risen to elite status in their groups or professions accentuates, in turn, the tendency to elitism in the elite opinion stream as a whole.

EXPERTISE AND ELITISM

Tension between the idea of political equality and the desirability of expertise is inherent in democracy, or at least present in all its recorded history. In the *Protagoras*, Plato has Socrates introduce his critique of democracy by comparing technical or professional knowledge with political ability. As paraphrased by Werner Jaeger in *Paideia*, Socrates marvels that "the cobbler, the tailor, and the carpenter should need special knowledge to practice their own honest trades, while the politician needed only a general and rather indefinite education to engage in politics, although his 'craft' dealt with much more important things." The implication, of course, is that politics should be headed by a class of political experts.[16]

Writing from a perspective much more favorable to democracy, Rousseau argued that as modern society became more and more complex, differences in expertise would lead inevitably to inequality and hierarchy, and ultimately to rule by the few. His solution was to oppose the kind of economic development that would make society any more complex than the simple, direct democracy he admired in the Swiss mountains.

In defending monarchy after the outbreak of the French Revolution, Edmund Burke (in his later, more elitist mode) wrote that the art of government was too complex for the average man, for whom it would always remain something of a mystery. But in *Rights of Man*, Thomas Paine replied that the process of representative government, as already operating in the United States, "diffuses such a body of knowledge throughout a nation on the subject of government as to explode ignorance and preclude imposition." Paine argued that because previous political revolutions had happened "within the atmosphere of a court, and never on the great floor of a nation," their instigators "took care to represent government as a thing made up of mysteries, which only themselves understood; and they hid from the understanding of the nation the only thing that was beneficial to know, namely, *that government is nothing more than a national association acting on the principles of society.*"[17]

Paine's italicizing of this last phrase points up the connection between the classical theory of politics as the setting of community standards applicable to everyone, and the possibility of rational choosing by a mass electorate. In this view society may be complex, and expertise may be needed to analyze its components, but the fundamental decisions that determine the shape of society concern values—that is, what kind of laws and habits the people should have.

In *Patterns of Anti-Democratic Thought*, David Spitz poses the issue as one of ends vs. means: "Consider, for example, the simple problem involved in the purchase of a house or automobile. To do either effectively it is not necessary for the ordinary man to become an architect or a bricklayer or a machinist or mechanic. On matters of technical competence he relies instead on the expert, who advises, performs, and when necessary repairs the house or the automobile. But the ordinary man himself makes the decision, both as to whether he should have the house or the automobile and which house or automobile it shall be, and who shall build or supply the house or automobile. This is the age-old and still central distinction between ends and means, values and techniques, policy and administration. The ordinary man decides what is to be done and who shall do it; the expert determines how it is to be done."[18]

Indeed, it is possible to turn Socrates' argument for expertise on its head. In his relatively simple society, it might be possible for a few gifted rulers to gain enough expertise to govern the *polis* in all its activities. But the more complex society becomes, the more experts are needed in more fields; and more and more experts know a smaller and smaller percentage of society as a whole. Highly complex societies like the United States are in a sense ungovernable, unless the entire citizenry is activated to govern itself.

Even in its own domain, expertise can mislead. Of its nature, expertise has a tendency to be conservative, almost static concerning its field. The history of various disciplines and professions is replete with revolutions of thought that had to be led by heretics, outsiders, and amateurs, because at any given time expertise is devoted to what is known about the present and past rather than the future.

Populism itself implies a belief in expertise. One aspect of optimism about people's ability to make decisions about their own affairs is optimism about their ability to call on experts to participate in such decisions. And economic populism implies a belief in the ability of more and more people to attain expertise in their own work.

In times when the standard-setting aspect of politics is eclipsed by the concept of politics as discretionary rule by elites, government by expertise gains in attraction. If government is seen as the solving of thousands of discrete, specialized problems, unconnected by overarching ideas or standards, then the political elite feels a drive to call in experts to recommend decisions on behalf of the people in each area of life, as did a recent secretary of agriculture, Bob Bergland, in 1977: "We want to know how much animal fat, how much sugar, how many eggs it's wise for a person to eat. Then we're going to build a new farm policy based on these truths."[19]

Few modern populists would share Rousseau's downright hostility to expertise, and to the increasing complexity that demands it in so many areas. For all their skepticism about the experts' tendency to elitism, most populists are optimistic about the ability of people to benefit from expert help, in individual and even political decision-making. With their pessimism about people's decision-making, as well as their bias toward discretionary rule rather than standard-setting, elitists often see expertise as a setter of goals as well as a finder of means.

INTEREST-GROUP ELITISM

With the coming of democracy, segments of the electorate naturally become of great interest to the political elite. In turn, members of these segments form groups and select leaders to express their views and interests to the political elite and to public opinion.

Whether the elite heading a given interest group is elitist or populist in its views is greatly influenced by the situation of that interest group with regard to political equality. If the interest group lacks elements of political equality, its leaders will tend to make populist arguments to the political elites and to the electorate. If the group has or attains a measure of political equality, it is more likely that the leaders of the interest group will shift toward arguments that are elitist with regard to the rank and file of the interest group.

While blacks lacked voting rights in much of the South, civil rights leaders were more likely to make the populist argument that once given such rights, blacks would handle them competently. But once those rights had been won, some of the same leaders argued that blacks could not exercise their vote competently enough to compete on equal terms with white voters. This implicitly elitist assumption with regard to blacks became the centerpiece of efforts to justify enhanced black representation by means of preferential redistricting.

Similarly, an association of textile producers arguing for tariffs or quotas against imported textiles is unlikely to be optimistic about the ability of its members to compete in a climate of equal opportunity with respect to foreign producers. To justify the preferential treatment of a tariff or quota, the interest group would of course make an argument that is elitist with regard to its members.

To the extent they lack political equality, then, interest groups are likely to be populist. To the extent equality is gained or exceeded, interest groups will tend to be pessimistic about the abilities of their members. When interest groups have significant power in a regime of political equality, interest-group elitism becomes a major factor in that society. As soon as an interest group reaches equality, the power of an interest-group elite tends to be enhanced it if adopts an attitude of pessimism concerning its members, and if it is able to spread that pessimism to other elites and to the popular opinion stream.

Interest-group elitism interacts with party elites of the sort inaugurated by Robert Walpole in England and carried to a high art form by paternalistic political machines such as Tammany Hall in New York and Richard Daley's Chicago. If, as Richard Jensen has written, Franklin D. Roosevelt in the New Deal brought the ethic of Tammany Hall to the nation at large, it is not surprising that mass-based interest groups became an integral part of the Democratic majority coalition of the New Deal era.

Developments in political science not only affirmed the legitimacy of interest-group elitism, but depicted it as the essence of political life. As mentioned in Chapter 4, the foundation was laid by Joseph Schumpeter's theory of democracy as a competition among elites for the affections of a passive and selfish electorate. Then in the late 1940s, the idea of government as negotiator among interest groups, far removed from the electorate, received a further boost from the revival of interest in the political theory of John C. Calhoun, the nineteenth-century politician and pro-slavery opponent of majority rule. In this climate, the classical view of politics as a debate among people who set community standards through legislation tends to give way to a vision of politics as a society-wide "consensus" arrived at principally by elite negotiations.

Interest-group elitism was by no means a monopoly of the Democratic party in twentieth-century America. Herbert Hoover, who in the early Depression resisted direct aid to people but promoted aid to corporations and other institutions through such proposals as the Reconstruction Finance Corporation, embodied institutional elitism to a much greater extent than did Roosevelt himself. One aspect of Keynesianism—the desire to stimulate the economy by putting money directly into the pockets of the people—had a much more populist root than anything in the Republican program of the 1930s. The Keynesians were not opposed to the humanitarian aspects of relief, but they also believed the use made by people of government aid would be more helpful to the economy than aid to business.

Once equality is achieved, the temptation to form interest groups that lobby for a larger share of the pie is always present. From then on, the power of such interest groups is closely related to the competition between populism and elitism among elites and in the popular opinion stream. In a climate where optimism about people's ability is widespread, talented elites are less likely to spend the time and effort needed to convince various groups that elite help is needed for them to survive, and the importance of interest-group elitism declines accordingly.

PROFESSIONAL AND GROUP ELITISM

A different kind of elitism may arise in a profession or group whose members possess elite status by virtue of such membership. Examples of such professions are law, science, investment banking, and college teaching in the United States; an example of such a group is graduates of Oxford and Cambridge in Britain.

Such a profession or group would generally be internally populist; that is, optimistic about the ability of its members to handle their own affairs. Elitism in such a group would tend to arise with regard to non-members of the group; that is, members of the elite group might be optimistic about their own ability to make decisions on behalf of non-members of the group, perhaps even on behalf of society as a whole.

Not surprisingly, this kind of elitism tends to wax and wane according to the status and internal self-confidence of the profession or group in question. Although such things are hard to quantify, one could venture that in the United States scientific elitism peaked around the 1940s and 1950s; educational elitism in the 1960s as the post-Sputnik focus on education and the post-war expansion of universities crested; and journalistic elitism in the 1960s and 1970s with the rise of network news and of confrontational investigative reporting of the sort that made folk heroes of two journalists in Watergate. Even more recently, the image of lawyers as *de facto* social legislators via the public-interest law suit and a reformist judiciary helped entice a flood of upwardly mobile students to attend law school.

Professional and group elitism is often closely intertwined with careerism. Careerists within an elite profession, after all, have two possible ways to advance their career: personal advancement within the group, and advancement of the group's importance within society. The latter half of the careerist agenda fits in with elitist theories of the group's ability to make decisions on behalf of others, though of course it is not the only reason for the existence of such beliefs.

The element of careerism increases conformity within the elite opinion stream. Part of qualifying for a professional or group elite, particularly such rigidly hierarchical elites as college teaching and prestige journalism, is the ability to fit in with the views of senior superiors who have virtually exclusive control over the entrant's fate. In a time when elitist ideas are widespread in the elite opinion stream, it could be as counterproductive for a young entrant to prestige journalism to express optimism about his audience as for a management trainee at General Motors to express optimism about the rank and file of the UAW. More normal in prestige journalism is the view of Av Westin, producer of the ABC news show "20/20" who said in 1982 that he and his staff produce his program under the assumption that "viewers bring zero interest and zero knowledge to our show."[20]

Elite professions have demanding entrance requirements. Years of graduate training are often only a start; such elite institutions as medicine, law firms, and (increasingly) prestige journalism have become noted for their demanding work weeks for beginners. People who have passed such an obstacle course know they have accomplished something the vast majority of the population could not. From there it is a short step to elitism, the belief that such well-tested elites are well able to make decisions on behalf of that majority.

INTERNAL ELITISM

Elite groups and professions tend to be so optimistic about their members that they often tend to be pessimistic about the people as a whole, at least by comparison with themselves. Interest-group elites in a regime of equality, by contrast, tend to be so pessimistic about their members that they often view the rest of society as a kind of collective elite, morally compelled by their superior status to divert resources to the interest group in question. But whether the rest of the community is viewed as superior or inferior to one's own group, the result of either elitism in policy terms is often surprisingly similar: diversion by the rest of the community of resources and/or power to the group in question. In democracy, the community as a whole must ratify the diversion, but the information and analysis that leads to such decisions is provided by elites.

Another kind of elitism is less directly involved with the community as a whole. This elitism is optimism about the ability of an elite to make decisions on behalf of the people within a given sector of society, concerning decisions involving that sector only. Examples would be managerial elitism in business, clerical elitism in religion, and the elitism of the officer corps in military life.

Because it is limited, this kind of internal elitism is more compatible with political populism than are other kinds of elitism. Many thoroughgoing populists would defend the need for orders to be obeyed without question in the army, or for courses of study at a university to be mapped out by scholars rather than by undergraduates. These examples involve, at least in part, an imbalance of expertise within a group that might well *require* inequality and/or elitism.

There could also be inequalities of standing. The owner of a grocery store could hire two people to sweep the floors, but his populism would hardly compel him to award each of them an equal say to his own in the running of the business. On the other hand, as mentioned in Chapter 2, elitist and populist theories of internal management have often contended for influence in business, with profound ripple effects in the political community as a whole.

Indeed, internal elitism has its greatest political effects by analogy, particularly when members of an elite generalize from their experience in the group to society as a whole. Clerical elitism may be highly defensible as a means of spreading the tenets of a faith to the believers, but when it tries to dictate to those believers in political matters, it turns into the political elitism known as clericalism. When a religious elite calls on the political elite to impose its authority on all people, believer and unbeliever alike, it adopts still another form of political elitism, establishmentarianism.

In transitions to equality from either monarchy or colonialism, so often fraught with political unrest or even chaos, military elites are especially likely to reason in this way—from the particular to the general. They contrast the order and efficiency within their own ranks with the unrest in society at large and are tempted to impose that order on the political realm. Anyone who might think the recent experiences of the post-colonial Third World are unique in this regard would do well to remember Cromwell's dismissal of Parliament in England, Bonapartism in France, and the battles between the Continental Congress and Continental Army in revolutionary North America.

In less dramatic circumstances, internal elitism has a tendency to interact with other kinds of elitism, contributing to the pessimism about people that often affects the elite opinion stream as a whole. Such factors as careerism, power worship, and arrogance are of course factors in elitism, as they are in other belief systems. But questionable motives on the part of ambitious people are unlikely to attain critical mass in the age of equality without strong reinforcement from sincerely elitist argumentation and belief, among the elites themselves and to some extent in public opinion as a whole.

CHAPTER 7

PUBLIC OPINION

POLITICAL POPULISM is optimism about the role of public opinion in deciding political issues.

Populism does not imply that every possible issue in life would benefit by being put to a vote. Indeed, part of populism's view of public opinion is optimism about the ability of public opinion to decide which of life's decisions *belong* in the area of political decision-making, and which other subjects belong in the private, non-political realm.

Put another way, political populism involves optimism about the role of public opinion in arriving at conclusions on those subjects which public opinion should help decide. It also believes that public opinion is competent to help decide what those subjects are.

Political populism should not be understood to mean that in a democracy, public opinion always prevails, or should prevail. Sometimes it gives way to other forces, such as determined resistance by society's elites. Sometimes this resistance is helpful. Public opinion is not always right, and is not even always populist; that is, it is not always optimistic about people's abilities in given areas.

Public opinion can of course change over time, so that its outlook at one moment can contradict its outlook at some other time. Such changeability does not lessen populism's optimism about public opinion. In fact, a major part of this optimism is the belief that public opinion can change for the better through debate, journalism, elections, and other practices associated with regimes of political equality.

Because of this belief, populism is more likely to be optimistic about the role of public opinion at the conclusion of a democratic debate than at its beginning. Populism in the context of democracy presumes the existence of free speech, free campaigning, and free votes. It is therefore less optimistic about the role of public opinion in communities where political elites have foreclosed one or more of these practices. This would of course particularly apply to a community where only one side of an issue is known—that is, where open debate has not yet begun or cannot take place at all.

Political elitism is pessimistic about the role of public opinion in deciding political issues. A political elitist could be a believer in presently recognized political equality, and therefore believe that as a moral imperative, public opinion should be freely expressed and be able to participate in political decision-making. But elitists tend to be pessimistic about the results of such participation, and as a consequence often favor ignoring public opinion in favor of decision-making by political and other elites.

When it comes to decision-making in "structural" issues in a democracy, or in a community considering the adoption of democracy, the major fight between populism and elitism is about the role of public opinion. Given their optimism about the role of public opinion in political decision-making, populists tend to favor institutions that let public opinion resolve a greater number of political questions than do elitists. Populists also tend to favor more channels for the expression of public opinion than do elitists, and are more likely to welcome technological and other developments that create such channels.

Political populists often favor direct voting on issues in various ways: binding initiative and referendum as exists in Switzerland and in nearly half of the United States; direct popular nomination of candidates, whether through party primaries or two-stage elections in which a second round of voting is held if no candidate gets a majority in the first; democratic decentralization, which provides more than one level of government for public opinion to affect; and separate election of the legislative and executive branches of government, which provides more than one branch of government for public opinion to affect.

Political elitists, by contrast, are more likely to favor centralized, parliamentary government, because it provides public opinion with only one level and one branch of government to affect, and because in parliamentary regimes the timing of elections is almost wholly at the discretion of political elites. In centralized parliamentary systems, furthermore, public opinion tends to have a much smaller role in selection of the contending political elites than in presidential systems. In other words, to become prime minister in most parliamentary systems, a person must first be selected by the political elites within his party.

LEGISLATIVE VS. EXECUTIVE

One irony of the split between legislative and executive is that the doctrine of separation of powers was developed in the eighteenth century by such thinkers as Montesquieu and Madison primarily in order to moderate and control public opinion, rather than to provide multiple channels for it. Early democratic populists, such as Roger Williams in Rhode Island and members of egalitarian state parties under the Articles of Confederation, favored unitary power centered in legislatures, with limited and often emasculated executives.

Given the origin of early drives for political equality in Britain and North America as revolts against the English monarchy, early populists naturally assumed that the executive branch was undemocratic and the chief threat to public opinion. Another factor was the classical view of John Locke and others mentioned in Chapter 3, which saw the heart of political life in the setting of community standards—that is, in the legislative aspect of politics.

Once it became clear that democracy in a jurisdiction larger than a city-state would involve major elements of representation, rather than government by direct vote or lot, the dominance of the classical standard-setting view of politics brought the legislative branch to the fore. This in turn created legislative elites.

The emergence of political elites in the first mass democracies was no surprise to anyone who had read earlier political philosophy. Rousseau was so suspicious of political elites that he opposed trying to extend democracy beyond the local level to a larger arena, where he knew representation, and the creation of political elites, was inevitable. Jefferson, for his part, devoted a good deal of his writing to the need of democratic society to educate its emerging political elites.

The surprise was that political elitism could lodge itself in the legislative branch, according to classical theory the most democratic part of democracy, as easily as anywhere else. The populist party in the early years of the Constitution, Jefferson's Democratic-Republicans, regarded the legislative branch, particularly the directly elected House of Representatives, as the bastion of the common people. The first national party system of the new republic, pitting the Jeffersonians against the elitist, pro-executive, pro-English Federalists, seemed to confirm the pro-legislative leanings of earlier populists.

But after 1812, the Federalists withered as a national opposition party, and in the weak presidencies of Madison and Monroe (1809–25), Congress gradually gained in power. According to Leonard D. White in *The Jeffersonians*, his study of governmental administration in the first third of the nineteenth century, "Congress became the dominant partner, whether in war or peace. The center of initiative and leadership passed to the House. It was concentrated in the office of the Speaker, and was supported by the nominating caucus, the legislative caucus, and the standing committees."[21]

The nominating caucus was the ultimate symbol of legislative supremacy, because it nominated the party's candidates for president. The erosion of executive power in the later Jeffersonian period parallelled the trend in Britain with the rise of Parliament and its increasing ability to dominate the King in selecting the "king's ministers."

But the increasingly powerful legislative elites met a sudden and major setback. In 1824, the Jeffersonian congressional caucus nominated William Crawford as its candidate for president, and presidential politics exploded in a way never to be reversed. Crawford finished far behind Andrew Jackson and John Quincy Adams in both popular and electoral votes, and the Electoral College failed to produce the required majority, sending the election to the House. In a last stab at legislative control of the presidency, the House elected the second-place candidate, John Quincy Adams, over Jackson and Crawford.

But the legislative elites had taken on not just the executive branch, but public opinion itself. Andrew Jackson made the elevation of the second-place Adams a symbol of injustice, riding the issue to election in 1828. From then on, the Electoral College was a mere mode of vote-counting; the presidency had become a popular institution. In the increasingly democratic-minded United States, that meant legitimacy and independence for the executive branch.

The fundamentally populist character of the strengthened executive might have been puzzling to the authors of the *Federalist* and to the other founders, including Jefferson, but the subsequent history of mass democracy has confirmed it. Virtually every period in which populist reform was on the agenda in the United States featured a populist-inclined executive fighting a more elitist-minded legislature. This is true of the presidency from Andrew Jackson to Ronald Reagan and tends to be equally true of populism at the state level, such as Governor Hiram Johnson's battle for direct democracy against the corporate-controlled California legislature. Even in Britain, with its gradually growing unity between legislative and executive, it was when a strong prime minister such as Peel or Gladstone emerged to dominate Parliament that populist reform, whether of an economic, political, or social nature, went forward most successfully.

An executive branch with a popular base independent of the body of legislators, constitutionally as in the United States or because of the personal dominance of a Gladstone, has a claim to represent directly all of the people in a way that a Speaker of the House or other legislative leaders do not. Furthermore, in a time when public opinion is in a mood for populist reform, it is easier for it to elect a single president or governor of its choice than to repopulate a numerous legislative body, with its power of incumbency and ties to the previous cycle's way of doing things.

REPRESENTATION

The rise of Andrew Jackson also meant that the victory of republicanism over direct democracy had not ended the argument about the role of public opinion at the national level. The Jacksonians elaborated the theory of popular sovereignty, which, they argued, could work through political leaders who possessed the quality of "genius." Genius was defined by the Jacksonian theorist George Bancroft as "the sympathetic character" by which the leader "was able with instinctive perception to read the soul of the nation." Ultimately, the power was that of the people, and the definition of political genius was the ability to read and implement public opinion.

So from Jackson on, the debate between political populists and political elitists was not simply the obvious one about direct democracy vs. delegated democracy, localism vs. centralism, which had defined the earlier debate (and has always persisted in some form); it was also an argument about the attitude of political elites toward public opinion. The Jacksonians and later populists took for granted the role of political elites in mass democracy, but argued that if political elites correctly regarded their role as the articulators and translators of public opinion, popular sovereignty could be as much of a reality as it had been in the Athens of direct voting and officeholding by lot. Elitists have argued that given the complexity not only of modern politics but of the modern world itself, and the resultant multiplicity of issues politics must address, the best public opinion can be expected to do is elevate political elites who in turn make the hard decisions of government.

PUBLIC OPINION AND COMPLEXITY

Particularly in the twentieth century, a time of global upheaval that has made isolationism all but impossible for most democracies, elitists have scored gains by arguing the inability of public opinion to understand complexity or address a multiplicity of problems. And it is true that Switzerland, the one populist democracy where public opinion can at any time overrule the political elites by direct voting, is also the one democracy that has consciously chosen not to have a foreign policy; it opted instead for peaceful isolation and non-involvement in alliances or other international political groups such as the United Nations and European Community.

But when personal leadership is needed in a democracy, populists have argued that public opinion tends to pick a leader whose character and values it trusts. At most times, such values would tend to include a respect for public opinion, rather than contempt for it. Three great crisis leaders of the United States—Abraham Lincoln, Woodrow Wilson, and Franklin Roosevelt—all embodied some measure of this respect for public opinion, certainly compared to their contemporary opponents.

Many populists, moreover, would deny that a multiplicity of issues makes public opinion irrelevant. V. O. Key, one of the few populist political scientists of this century, argues that the role of public opinion should be seen not as "one in which by some mysterious means a referendum occurs on every major issue," but as a series of dikes that channel the discussion among political elites, leaving them some discretion in details but circumscribing the bounds of action.[22]

ACTIVATING PUBLIC OPINION

Few populists would argue that public opinion can never be passive or inert, particularly in societies, nominally democratic or not, that have little sense of popular participation in political decision-making. James Bryce, for one, mentions the activating of public opinion as a key milestone of progress in modern democratic culture.

Public opinion is least likely to be activated when it sees little possibility of prevailing. In the words of J. R. Lucas in *The Principles of Politics*, "By conferring on subjects the possibility of participation, we make them forfeit the status of spectators and take on the more responsible one of agents: and correspondingly change the logical level of their arguments from that of critical skepticism to that of serious consideration of practical possibilities. . . . Political liberty makes political reasoning realistic, cogent, and likely to be effective."[23]

Again and again, public opinion changes when it is confronted no longer with a hypothetical possibility, but with actual decision-making. For years, polls in the United Kingdom found overwhelming opposition to entering the Common Market. As soon as the issue was submitted to binding referendum, public opinion reversed itself in response to the resulting debate. In the United States, for many years prior to 1980, Edward Kennedy was picked as the American people's favorite candidate for president. When he announced his candidacy in 1979, he had within weeks dropped far behind his opponents in both parties.

These verdicts of the British and American electorates may have been right or wrong. Less in dispute is that in each case, public opinion was activated by the imminence of democratic decision-making. Populists argue that political equality is more likely to activate public opinion than is an oligarchy, and that in regimes of equality public opinion is most likely to be activated when it knows it will participate in the decision made.

POPULIST POLITICAL REFORMS

The development of political institutions that give greater outlet to public opinion in mass democracy is closely tied to the history of the United States. Something like the political party system first appeared in England, while initiative and referendum was pioneered in Switzerland, but most other populist political reforms had their beginnings in the world's oldest mass democracy.

Part of the reason for this is the United States' early commitment to wider and wider extension of voting rights. But extension of the franchise to new segments of the population is, properly speaking, a growth in political equality, in which optimism about the proposed recipients may or may not be a central motive. As emphasized repeatedly in these pages, populism and political equality often reinforce each other but are not identical. As one example where one advanced with little help from the other, extension of political rights to black slaves at the time of the Civil War was not accompanied by much optimism about blacks, even among abolitionists. Even when he issued the Emancipation Proclamation, Abraham Lincoln was not optimistic about the ability of blacks to exercise the political rights he favored for them. His position on blacks was analogous to George Washington's concerning republican government itself: belief in political equality as a moral right, but pessimism as to its recipients' ability to handle it once granted.

Granting of political rights to new groups has, nevertheless, often been accompanied by populist political reforms. When the *definition* of public opinion is being widened, there often is a search for more *outlets* for public opinion.

There have been four major periods of populist political reform in the United States since 1789. The first or Jeffersonian period took place mainly in the 1790s and in 1800 and 1801, and saw the following developments: the formation of the first true opposition party; the organization of the first grass-roots party; and the first peaceful change of power from an incumbent party to an opposition party based exclusively on election results.

The second or Jacksonian period took place in the 1820s and 1830s and saw: the democratization of the presidency and its escape from legislative control; the first policy veto of the democratized presidency, Jackson's veto of the rechartering of the Second Bank of the United States in 1832; and, following the veto, the formation of the Democrats and Whigs as the first modern mass-based two-party system. One key development of the 1830s, the invention of national party conventions, ratified the executive's independence from the legislative and gave the national party system an autonomy never since lost.

These first two periods of populist political reform were associated with partisan realignments: the displacement of the Federalists by Jefferson's Democratic-Republicans in 1800, and the triumph of the Jacksonian Democrats in 1828–36. In each case, the victorious party in the realignment had a virtual monopoly of contemporary populism, while its opponents, the Federalists and Whigs, were clearly elitist in overall orientation. The two more recent periods of major populist advance have had a bipartisan configuration.

Between 1900 and 1920, the third or Progressive movement of populist reform swept through both parties and all levels of government. As Robert Kelley has pointed out in *The Cultural Pattern in American Politics*, it was so comprehensive that it resembled the period of the American Revolution much more than a party realignment. The Progressive period saw the following populist political reforms: enactment of the direct party primary for governor, Congress, and dozens of state and local offices; the first presidential primaries; direct election of senators; initiative, referendum, and recall in about half of the states; and enfranchisement of women.

The big loser among political institutions in the Progressive period was the political party, which had started as an instrument of populists in the Jeffersonian and Jacksonian periods, but had taken on a clearly elitist cast in the eyes of populist reformers by the late nineteenth century. The two movements that laid the basis for the Progressive revolution, the Mugwumps and the Populists, had virtually nothing in common in their cultural background or economic platforms. But they agreed totally in their commitment to such populist *political* reforms as the secret ballot and direct primary to break up what they saw as an elitist alliance of party bosses and corrupt businessmen at every level of government.

The big institutional winner of this period was the presidency. Starting with William McKinley (1897–1901), every president had to deal with complex, contentious issues of foreign policy, which increased public opinion's desire for the personal leadership that the presidency has often fulfilled. The rise of the presidential primary continued the trend toward democratization of the office, and it is perhaps no accident that it was at the culmination of these developments that Woodrow Wilson took the Gladstonian-populist tradition of optimism about public opinion worldwide, with his campaign for self-determination in Europe following the American intervention in World War I.

The final or modern wave of populist political reform began in the 1960s and may still be continuing. It included the civil rights revolution, in particular the enfranchisement of Southern blacks by the Voting Rights Act of 1965; the dominance of the preferential primary in presidential politics beginning in 1972; and the use of the state-level initiative and referendum for radical policy reform, especially California's Proposition 13 in 1978. In more recent years has come a movement for term limitation for state and federal legislators. As in the Progressive period, the latter part of the modern period has seen an upsurge in presidential evangelism of democratic values on the international stage, beginning with President Carter's human-rights campaign and continuing with President Reagan's democracy initiative.

The present wave of political populism has not only had major impact on both parties, but has been accompanied by major devel-

opments in what might be called the "private" political culture—
the shaping and expression of public opinion itself. These developments began before the 1960s with the rise of split-ticket voting, of
television as the dominant medium of national and statewide politics, and of public opinion polling. As in the Progressive period, a
major loser has been the political party, as candidates and public
opinion have found new and more direct modes of communicating
with each other. Elitist opposition and resistance to all these developments has not only been bipartisan, as in the Progressive period,
but bi-ideological. Liberal and conservative elitists who agree on
little else tend to share a generally negative view of the presidential
primary system, split-ticket voting, initiative and referendum, polling, and (perhaps above all) the thirty-second political "spot." Since
the recent period has been one in which the elite opinion stream
has been far more elitist than the norm of American history, most of
these populist developments have gone virtually without articulate
defense. They all, nevertheless, appear to be here to stay.

For both the modern period and the Progressive period, it is
important to keep in mind the distinction between political
populism—optimism about the role of public opinion in
democracy—and other types of populism, such as economic populism and social populism. The Progressive period and the present
period have seen many cross-cutting currents in popular debate,
and developments that increase political populism can easily coincide with leanings to elitism in economic or social policy. Practitioners of populist reform in these two periods have come from
both parties and from varied cultural roots, and have often been
elitist on the social and economic issues that have made up a large
share of the debate. What is hard to deny is that, regardless of the
mixed character of these practitioners, the reforms and developments of the two periods have brought greater power and more
weapons to the expression of public opinion—so much so that,
apart from Switzerland, it is difficult to find a democratic country
that had even *one* period of populist political reform comparable to
the first twenty years and the most recent thirty years of this
century.

BARRIERS TO POPULIST REFORM

Important and striking as these waves of reform in the United
States are, their seeds are present in the nation's two-century-old
Constitution, which establishes such features as separation of the
presidency from Congress, decentralization, and the possibility of
grass-roots amendment of the Constitution. The Founders did not
anticipate the rise of the party system, but they provided enough
outlets for public opinion that party elites could always be ousted if
they drifted too far away from public opinion. As one example,
direct election of U.S. senators would have been unlikely without
the Constitution's provision for bypassing the senators themselves,
via a (never-invoked) convention called by the states.

These possibilities are rarely present in democracies that have
adopted unwritten constitutions or have vested all possibility of
amendment in political elites. In parliamentary systems, such
elites tend to be party elites not directly accountable to public
opinion except in general elections every few years.

The kind of system that most limits the role of public opinion is a
parliamentary system that operates by proportional representation.
Proportional representation awards seats to parties in accord with
the percentage of votes they receive in the parliamentary election.
Its proponents argue that it is the system most faithful to public
opinion, since a party that gains 10 percent of the vote gets 10
percent of the seats, rather than few or none as in the British and
American "winner-take-all" systems.

But in reality, proportional representation sets up incentives for
fragmentation of power among ideological, regional, and special-
interest political elites. This fragmentation makes it difficult if not
impossible for any one party to win a majority mandate; and the
makeup of the government coalition is determined by the incessant
maneuvering of party leaders. In post-war Italy and in the French
Fourth Republic, governments changed on average every few
months. In the Federal Republic of Germany, which has a partially
proportional system and whose partisan voting patterns are highly

stable, the only times a party has lost power to another party has been through a change of allegiance by a coalition member, usually the Free Democrats, a minuscule middle-of-the-road party that receives 5–10 percent of the national vote. In stable Germany no less than unstable Italy, public opinion finds it difficult to determine the government directly.

In France, the Gaullists who overthrew the Fourth Republic in 1958 established a strong presidency with a seven-year term, but made it difficult for the president to govern without the support of Parliament. While the executive and legislative have therefore not achieved the separation that exists in the United States, the Gaullists' abolition of proportional representation and requirement of an absolute majority for election to the presidency have ended the incessant elite maneuvering within fragmented parliaments characteristic of the Fourth Republic and present-day Italy.

And in Japan, the intermittent flirtation by the ruling Liberal Democratic party with holding the equivalent of a primary for party leadership—tantamount to a primary for prime minister— suggests that elite control of institutional change does not preclude populist political reform even in a seemingly closed parliamentary system. But the tendency of political elites to resist new outlets for public opinion, and the absence of provisions for grassroots amending of most democratic constitutions, make a wave of populist reform similar to those experienced by the United States unlikely. Such gestures as referenda on divisive issues (Common Market in Britain, divorce in Italy, NATO membership in Spain) are more likely to be episodic, and dictated less by populist sentiment than by the desire of political elites to survive sharp splits in public opinion.

POPULIST LEADERSHIP AND PUBLIC OPINION

It is a commonplace that successful political leaders in democracies are able to set up strong rapport with public opinion, which in turn entrusts them with great leverage on the rest of the political elites.

Robert Kelley writes of Gladstone that after 1859, he "ruled Parliament through the electorate. He was imposed upon the oligarchies in Lords and Commons by social forces coming from every direction. 'Gladstone exercises such a sway over the constituencies,' observed the Duke of Argyll in 1881 in a private letter, 'that the members are afraid to call their souls their own.' "[24]

Leaders who attain such mastery while privately holding the electorate in contempt do exist. But more often, as in the case of Gladstone, Lincoln, and Wilson, to name three, part of the attraction of public opinion to a democratic leader is based on his attraction to it. Public opinion's affection is far more likely to seek out a political leader if that affection is visibly reciprocated. Gladstone was not shy about expressing this view, for example during his successful drive to enfranchise rural laborers in the Reform Act of 1884: "[W]e are firm in the faith that the people may be trusted—that the voters under the Constitution are the strength of the Constitution."[25]

Gladstone started as a Tory opposed to extension of the franchise, but during his long career, he gradually reversed his view of public opinion, according to Kelley: "He had come to the view that the ordinary man had both the intellectual capacity to understand great issues and the moral character to act rightly upon them. When he spoke to his audiences, he assumed that they were serious and reflective. His speeches moved freely over all areas of statecraft, as if they were given on the floor of Commons itself. . . . He gave them the sense that they were being invited to join him in making moral judgments on public events of worldwide importance. He appealed confidently to a sense of compassion he was sure was in them—and which, perhaps, they therefore felt. The ordinary man standing in Gladstone's audiences was made to feel as though he had become a classless man, a disinterested man, a moral agent in the world."[26]

The great democratic war leaders—Pericles, Lincoln, Wilson, Roosevelt, Churchill—have all been praised for their ability to rally their electorates by their eloquence. But eloquence involves content as well as style, and a prominent theme of all these leaders, whatever their private reservations, was the superiority of democracy and self-government to the dictatorial systems of the war enemy. Lincoln is described by his biographer Benjamin Thomas as "realizing that the function of a political leader in a democracy is not to impose his will, but to help the people to decide wisely for themselves."[27]

Populist leadership in politics implies not only rapport with public opinion, but an almost ideological belief in the competence of public opinion as the basis of democratic life.

CHAPTER 8

ISSUES

PUBLIC OPINION in a democracy has two main subjects: issues and candidates. Within public opinion, the popular opinion stream tends to focus on issues as an end, while the elite opinion stream is more likely to focus on the rise or fall of candidates as an end. In other words, each opinion stream is interested in both candidates and issues, but the popular opinion stream is interested in candidates mainly insofar as they contribute to the resolution of issues, while members of the elite opinion stream are more likely to view issues in the light of their effect on candidates.

By their nature, elites are fascinated with success and excellence. Leaders in their own fields, they often value political leadership as an end in itself, and in assessing political figures are far less likely to see such figures as vehicles for ideas than to see ideas as a "platform" for an aspiring or incumbent leader to stand on. This attitude can be seen in many elites—for example, the media elite's oft-remarked focus on the "horse race" aspect of politics at the expense of issues—but the focus on personal careers as the end of politics is understandably most intense among the political elites themselves.

Members of the popular opinion stream do not have this luxury. Some may be interested in a member of a political elite in the same sense as in a sports or movie star, but in their role as components of public opinion they are far more likely to be interested in the careers of political leaders as disposers of the sorts of issues that can affect their daily lives in significant ways.

TYPES OF ISSUES

What are these issues? For the most part, they deal with the setting of community standards, the combatting of public evils, or some combination of the two.

The setting of community standards is at the root of all significant issues, since a public evil cannot even be defined, much less combatted, unless the community has a previously established standard in the area of life in question. A community, moreover, often concludes that a public evil, or even a cluster of public evils, can be combatted only by some action regarding standards. Such actions include setting, repealing, modifying, or enforcing more strictly one or more community standards.

For these reasons and others, the classical view of politics (discussed in Chapter 3) is that the decision on standards is a community's ultimate act of political self-definition. But a community standard, once set, does not necessarily give rise to an issue, even if the standard in question is important. The provision in the U. S. Constitution mandating election of the House of Representatives by direct vote of the electorate is an important standard (and has been far-reaching in its global impact). But since it has never come under serious public question, this standard has not given rise to an issue in the United States except at the time it was legislated by the founders.

Historical situations such as the founding are the only times when public evils are not necessarily involved in the origin of issues. This is because a group of people coming together to found a new nation, or a new political order, may insert a provision either in reaction to a public evil—say, the weakness of the United States government under the Articles of Confederation—or simply because it is expressing a belief, previously abstract but now embodied in a community standard.

Once the community's political system is established, an issue is invariably triggered by widespread perception of a public evil. If the public evil is believed to be a public evil by both sides of the debate, the issue is what political scientists have named a valence issue. If the debate is in large measure about whether or not the social condition in question *is* a public evil, it is a values issue. (This term is used in preference to the term standards issue because of the earlier point that any widely agreed-on public evil must be one because it violates some kind of community standard, and thus in this important sense all issues are standards issues.)

A public evil is a kind of social condition. If a condition is seen as good, it is unlikely to become an issue. Even if a condition is seen as clearly evil, it does not necessarily give rise to a *public* issue—that is, an evil that becomes a subject of political decision-making. It could be a private evil, such as the death of a loved one by natural causes. To become an issue, the condition must be seen as an evil that affects or is capable of affecting the public at large, or some significant segment of it. The clearest examples of such an evil would be an economic depression or a threat of enemy attack.

Because these are *clear* examples of public evils—social conditions which both sides of debate usually acknowledge to be public evils as a starting point of debate—they usually take the form of valence issues. The debate is mainly about how to combat the widely acknowledged evil in question.

A values issue, by contrast, involves a social condition which one side views as a public evil and the other side does not, and where a significant share of the debate is about the nature of this social condition. Such issues have included slavery, public drinking, abortion, and pornography.

These examples make clear that over time, a values issue can turn into a valence issue, and vice versa, and that an issue stops being an issue when the public evil in question is eliminated, or when public opinion stops regarding it as a public evil. In the Northern states, American slavery evolved from a values issue—is it evil or not?—into a valence issue—how quickly and by what means can it be eliminated?—and then into a non-issue, with the eradication of chattel slavery in North America following the Civil War.

Public drinking was widely accepted early in the republic, and was not really an issue. When the Temperance movement arose, it became a values issue. As this movement gained, it succeeded in turning it from a values issue into a valence issue, and finally succeeded in enacting the Eighteenth Amendment as a national community standard. When the new standard was widely violated and scorned, the violation itself came to be seen as a public evil. Following the repeal of the national standard by the Twenty-first Amendment, public drinking stopped being a national issue because, in most sections of the country, public opinion had come to regard it as at most a private evil.

Just as a social condition cannot become an issue unless public opinion, or a significant segment of it, comes to regard it as a public evil, so in determining whether an issue is a values issue or a valence issue, public opinion is the variable, not the inner nature of the social condition itself. Even in the case of a classic valence issue—the threat of enemy attack—a major segment of public opinion can side with the attacker, as appears to have happened in Austrian public opinion regarding Germany's *Anschluss* in 1938. If a major segment of public opinion decides an invasion is more likely to fulfill community standards than violate them, even the threat of invasion can be a values issue rather than a valence issue. If public opinion as a whole accepts invasion, then the threat of invasion is a non-issue, and annexation generally results.

ANSWERS TO ISSUES

Public opinion, and particularly the popular opinion stream, judges political elites primarily by their success or failure at dealing with conditions it sees as public evils—that is, with issues. One way for a political elite to deal with an issue is to deny that the social condition in question *is* a public evil. This can be successful if the issue in question is or becomes a values issue—that is, if there is a significant segment of public opinion that does not regard the social condition as an evil, or can be convinced that it is not.

Another approach is to argue that while the issue in question *is* a public evil, it is caused by forces beyond present political control. This also can be successful, particularly if the other side of the debate agrees with this premise or advocates a solution to the issue that public opinion judges unacceptable.

The most effective way for a political elite to handle an issue is to provide an answer to the issue. An answer to an issue is one which ends, moves toward ending, or has the prospect (in the eyes of public opinion) of ending or reducing the public evil in question.

In every democracy, public opinion judges incumbent political elites on their handling of issues, and especially on whether they provide answers to issues. If an issue remains important through the entire term of an elected administration, both the incumbents and its challengers are then evaluated on their handling of the issue. Although failure to provide an answer to an important issue may not defeat or even hurt the incumbents, depending on the course of the debate and the performance of the challengers, it is hard to imagine an unanswered issue failing to defeat or at least hurt the incumbents if the challengers do provide an answer that seems more plausible to public opinion. In the case of an important issue, the popular opinion stream is highly unlikely to reward an incumbent elite for a failure that has lasted the term of its office, given a plausible alternative.

STAGFLATION AS AN ISSUE

In the United States in the 1970s, an economic issue arose and came to dominate much of the political debate in that decade and into the early 1980s. The issue can be summed up by a word invented at the time to describe it: stagflation. It involved historically high rates of inflation, sometimes 10 percent or more, accompanied by stagnant rates of economic growth compared to the previous decade and the post-World War II period as a whole.

Incumbent political elites, first the Nixon-Ford administration and later the Carter administration, suffered in popularity because of this issue. Other issues were important in the 1976 and 1980 elections, but polls taken at the time showed low grades for the incumbent elites in their handling of economic issues, and Presidents Ford and Carter suffered unusually strong challenges within their own parties and were eventually denied election, the first incumbent nominees to lose since 1932. By his election day President Ford had improved his standing on the economy and inflation had become fairly low, but few historians would deny that stagflation was involved in his defeat, and even more clearly in the defeat of President Carter in 1980.

As the presidential campaign season got under way in late 1979, Carter trailed far behind his chief challenger, Senator Edward Kennedy, in polls taken among Democratic voters. This situation soon changed, due in part to the performance of Kennedy as a candidate and in part to the eruption of the Iranian hostage crisis. But economics by no means disappeared from the debate between Carter and Kennedy.

The Kennedy campaign, in fact, had its origin in the issue of stagflation. Not only did it make Carter vulnerable to a challenge within his own party, it clearly made him vulnerable in the general election, and this realization added greatly to Kennedy's potential support base among Democratic elites. In August 1979, as double-digit inflation continued month after month and economic growth fell far below 1978 levels, Carter fired his Treasury secretary and appointed a new chairman of the Federal Reserve after shifting the previous incumbent, William Miller, into the Treasury vacancy.

In October, the new chairman of the Fed, Paul Volcker, announced a tough anti-inflationary policy based on tight money. Interest rates rose, then fell back, but inflation remained high. In early 1980, the annualized monthly rate of inflation went as high as 18 percent. (Inflation for the year proved to be 12.4 percent.)

Carter's attempt to answer the issue was not producing results. But the Kennedy campaign, reeling from a series of unrelated setbacks, did not attempt to provide a clear answer of its own, perhaps counting on public disgust with stagflation to produce negative voting without the need for a clear alternative. Kennedy did hint at some interest in wage and price controls, but his campaign did not emphasize this as a possible answer to the issue of stagflation.

Carter took the lead in Democratic polls and won the New Hampshire primary. By the time of the crucial Illinois primary a few weeks later, he was achieving landslide margins. "The reason a president is able to run on an 18 percent inflation rate," Carter's Illinois campaign manager Larry Hanson explained at the time, "is that no presidential candidate has presented any viable alternatives on economics."

Carter had virtually clinched renomination, but the inflation rate was higher than ever, and Iran had ceased to be an acknowledged Carter strong point, as his administration failed to provide an answer to an issue that the president himself had decided to emphasize. Kennedy began to win primaries, and Carter's support started to fall in match-ups against the certain Republican nominee, Ronald Reagan. In the spring, Carter imposed credit controls on the economy and Volcker simultaneously raised interest rates. A short, sharp recession followed, but Carter had more explicitly adopted as his own answer the tight-money policy earlier begun by his newly appointed Fed chairman.

Reagan, meanwhile, had answers of his own. He advocated a 30 percent tax cut over three years and restraint on domestic spending (largely unspecified) as his answers to stagflation. His Republican opponents in early primaries agreed on unspecified spending restraint but did not emphasize tax cuts as an answer to the public evil of stagflation.

Neither Reagan nor the other Republicans mentioned tight money as part of the answer to stagflation. By not seriously challenging the Carter-Volcker tight-money policy, the Republicans in a sense made this answer bipartisan. In turn, Carter announced a new plan of budget austerity that, in effect, made bipartisan the Republican advocacy of spending restraint. The part of Reagan's answer that Carter decided to challenge was the 30 percent tax cut. This ensured that a major part of the 1980 economic debate would be about Reagan's support of a tax cut, which was the most explicit part of his answer to the issue of stagflation.

Reagan's advocacy of a tax cut was most aggressive in the period between his defeat in the Iowa caucus in January and his victory in the New Hampshire primary in late February. As a result of his big victory in that primary, and also because of a change of campaign management on primary day, his campaign adopted a more cautious attitude to tax cutting after New Hampshire.

But his opponents, first George Bush in the remainder of the primaries and then Carter in the general election, kept the tax cut in the campaign by strongly attacking the idea as inflationary and (in Bush's phrase) "voodoo economics." Since there was no disagreement among the three on the remaining answers to stagflation—spending restraint and tight money—the tax cut part of Reagan's answer remained for public opinion the chief line of demarcation between Reagan and his opponents for the remainder of the election year.

That Reagan won the nomination and the election by solid margins does not imply that his advocacy of a tax cut as his most noticeable and controversial answer to the issue of stagflation made the difference. Other major issues were involved, especially the continuing Iranian hostage issue, a universally acknowledged public evil, and President Carter's inability to find an answer for it.

What is undeniable is that the issue of stagflation set the scene for Carter's defeat and that, unlike Kennedy, Reagan benefited enormously from the issue's prominence in the campaign. His advocacy of a tax cut was the major cutting edge not only of his program, but of his opponents' attacks on his program. That he benefited from the stagflation issue and carried every region of the country suggests strongly that public opinion found his answer to the issue more acceptable than that of Carter, who was hurt above all by the fact that he had had four years to grapple with stagflation and had failed (in the view of public opinion) to provide an answer of his own.

DIVERGENCE OF OPINION STREAMS

If a poll had been taken on the two candidates' handling of stagflation in the elite opinion stream alone, Carter would have done
considerably better than he did in the popular opinion stream. He
might even have won such a poll, although many who would have
sided with him on the economy might well have voted against him
for other reasons.

Similarly, Carter would have scored far better in the elite opinion
stream for his performance in the two candidates' important late-
October debate, much of which focused on the economy. This was
underlined by widespread puzzlement among political, media, and
other elites when a call-in poll conducted by ABC showed Reagan a
strong winner of the debate. Some tried to dismiss the ABC poll as
unscientific, which it was, but scientific tracking polls in the days
following the debate confirmed a strong movement in public opinion
toward Reagan.

Why such an apparent gulf between the popular and elite opinion streams on the answers of the two candidates, in the debate and
especially on the pivotal economic issue of stagflation?

First, content. Beginning with the 1960s, the elite opinion
stream had become more elitist in its views while the popular
opinion stream had become more populist. Compared to the 1950s,
when the division of belief among elites was not very different from
the division among public opinion as a whole—President
Eisenhower, for example, enjoyed wide popularity among both
opinion streams—the more recent period has seen a number of
issues and candidates where the two opinion streams react in
opposite ways.

On the subject of personal taxation, which emerged as the major
clash of answers between Reagan and Carter on the issue of stagflation, the basic arguments were tacitly located along populist-elitist
lines. The key *practical* question about a big tax cut is: how will
people behave if given a much greater proportion of the nation's
income stream? Reagan in effect said the people would generate

strong growth without inflation. Carter in effect said the people would take the extra money and bid up prices, which were already growing at a double-digit annual rate.

Because of the greater than normal elitist leanings of the elite opinion stream in the modern period, Carter's warnings had greater appeal to America's elites in 1980 than they did to public opinion as a whole. Even among those elites sympathetic to economic stimulus via tax cutting, the overwhelming preference was for corporate tax cuts rather than personal tax cuts. This was the belief of George Bush and other Republican critics of Reagan. The tacit argument was that corporate elites would make good use of an increase in their share of the national income stream, while individual taxpayers benefiting from across-the-board personal tax cuts would not. The year following the election, Reagan's own budget director, David Stockman, echoed this view of elitist Republicans when he said the broad personal tax cut was a "Trojan horse," tolerated by its advocates as a necessary evil to make possible tax cuts for the rich.

ELITE INCREMENTALISM

A second reason why elite opinion was so much more likely to favor Carter's handling of stagflation than was public opinion as a whole is its frequent tendency to incrementalism. Members of elites in a meritocratic society have usually attained their status by mastering the present status quo, whatever that happens to be. Proposals such as a deep tax cut or radical tax reform imply a rejection and overturn of the present system, under which elites have prospered and in which they tend to be comfortable.

Even in periods in which elites are not unusually elitist, they tend to be reluctant to embrace radical change and the rejection of their own success stories this implies. A Jacksonian, reformist Democratic tax cutter of the nineteenth century, Samuel Tilden, noted this tendency in 1884 when he argued that "All history shows that reforms in government must not be expected from those who sit serenely on the social mountain-tops enjoying the benefits of the existing order of things."[28]

Thus elites of whatever kind have a tendency to admire the stability of the "me-too" elections that have frequently characterized the post-war politics of the Federal Republic of Germany and other countries of Northern Europe. These elections are not just a tacit endorsement of the status quo under which elites have prospered, they also deny a major policy role to the popular opinion stream in the only real opportunity accorded to it by parliamentary government to influence the political elites.

ISSUES VS. STYLE

A third reason for the elite preference of Carter involved the styles of the two candidates. As noted earlier, all decisions of public opinion have to do with either issues or candidates. When evaluating a candidate, public opinion considers the candidate's quality and his position on issues.

These two elements of candidate appeal are often analyzed as if they were separate from each other, but in fact they are difficult to separate. A voter oriented toward issues will look at the quality of a candidate—his biography, speaking ability, campaign advertising, and all the rest—with an eye toward how the quality of the candidate will affect his ability to provide answers to issues. A voter oriented toward candidates will appraise the candidate's answers to issues in terms of how the content and delivery of those answers affect the candidate's overall quality. As noted early in this chapter, the first type of voter is more likely to be found in the popular opinion stream, the second in the elite opinion stream.

As candidates, Carter and Reagan both had appeal, but Carter's appeal was more congenial to the elite opinion stream. He was an incrementalist, he had great respect for expertise, he stressed the complexity and intractability of problems, he worked long hours, studied the details of issues exhaustively, and could recite facts and figures from his reading with authority and precision. These qualities are widely admired in the elite opinion stream, particularly as it is influenced by careerism.

Reagan, by contrast, tended toward radical solutions, argued that issues were basically simple and understandable to average voters, worked in a nine-to-five pattern, delegating detailed analysis to others, was weak on facts and figures, and preferred homilies and anecdotes in his speaking style. All these elements are unappealing to the elite opinion stream, particularly one that is in an elitist and incrementalist phase. And even when it is not in such a phase, the elite opinion stream tends to be interested in answers to issues as they affect candidate quality, rather than the reverse. All these factors help explain why the better informed and more successful an observer was, the more likely he was to underestimate Reagan's political ability.

The cleavage between the two opinion streams on candidate quality in recent years has been particularly clear in the phenomenon of the "gaffe." A gaffe is a misstatement or lapse in taste by a candidate. In the elite opinion stream, gaffes are taken seriously, and a series of gaffes can even disqualify a candidate in the minds of many elite voters. By contrast, gaffes have little or no effect on the popular opinion stream, which is always the vast majority of public opinion. The main way in which a gaffe can hurt a candidate with public opinion is when a candidate and his campaign, such as Gary Hart in 1984, appear to overreact or become visibly demoralized by a gaffe. Because most candidates and their advisors are members of the elite opinion stream, this often happens. But since Reagan, as a candidate, was well above average in his ability to take gaffes in stride, they hurt him very little in his career.

ANSWER TO STAGFLATION

Upon election, Reagan proceeded to implement his answer to stagflation: tax cuts, domestic spending restraint, and a continuation of

Carter's tight-money policy at the Federal Reserve. The policy did not achieve quick results. Inflation remained at 9 percent in 1981, and by the mid-term election of November 1982 the nation was only beginning to emerge from a much more severe recession than the one Carter presided over in 1980. Unemployment reached nearly 11 percent and the Democrats scored a twenty-six-seat gain in the House elections.

But in 1983 and 1984, a strong recovery took place while inflation fell to around 4 percent in each year. In 1984, with Reagan up for re-election, real GNP grew nearly 7 percent and unemployment fell to a little more than 7 percent, approximately where it was when Reagan took office. Reagan's popularity recovered from its 1982 lows and he was re-elected by a record margin, losing only thirteen electoral votes. According to exit polls, the leading factor in Reagan's landslide was public approval of his handling of the economy.

Many objections could be (and were) made to Reagan's performance on the economy: the defeat of inflation was due to Carter's appointee, Volcker, or to declines in international energy prices; the recession was more severe than needed to curb inflation; the budget deficit had reached record proportions; much of Reagan's initial progress in tax cutting and budget cutting had been eroded later in his term; average GNP growth and unemployment figures in his term were worse than under Carter; and so on. For public opinion, these points, however valid, were irrelevant. Reagan had advocated an answer to stagflation, and by November 1984 the United States had no stagflation. For the popular opinion stream, at least for that segment of it that voted on economic issues, this was decisive.

In the 1970s, as stagflation persisted and worsened, it grew as an issue because it grew as a public evil that was capable of affecting more and more lives. To say that the popular opinion stream was issue-oriented, in the sense that more and more of its members were willing to cast their ballots on the issue of the economy, is an understatement. It would be more correct to say that fewer and fewer members of the popular opinion stream could afford *not* to be oriented toward this issue. By the time of the 1980 election, the perception of stagflation as a public evil had given economics a more central place in American politics than at any time since the 1930s, and public opinion was judging candidates on their handling of this issue more than on any other factor.

By 1984, having in the view of public opinion provided an answer to the issue, there was no way that Reagan would not have benefited in his overall approval rating and electability. But since stagflation was no longer a public evil, there was no inherent reason why the economy should have dominated the election. True, the Republicans would claim credit for having ended stagflation, but in 1984 neither it nor any other economic question need have been a major point of argument between the two parties. When Democratic presidents achieved fast economic growth in the 1960s, Republican challengers did not focus on economic issues in 1964 or 1968. It was not in their interest to do so. When one issue is for some reason resolved, the natural tendency of politics is to move on to some other—sometimes one not so favorable to the incumbents who successfully resolved the dominant issue or issues of the previous period. Under President James Polk (1845–49), the Jacksonian Democrats enacted all their programs and began to achieve their long-held goals of broad-based economic growth and vast territorial expansion. Yet they lost the election of 1848 and eventually their majority status because this very growth and expansion raised a new question which they were not able to handle: would slavery grow and expand as well?

Unlike the Whigs of 1848 and the Republicans of 1968, the Democrats in 1984 chose to campaign mainly on economic issues, directly challenging Reagan's handling of the economy, his greatest area of success with public opinion. Since this was not, in objective terms, a promising strategy, the main motive of Democratic elites in pursuing this strategy was probably deep conviction. This conviction, in turn, was shaped by the especially elitist views in the elite opinion stream and by American elites' persistent tendency to underestimate the effectiveness of Reagan, for all the reasons mentioned earlier.

DEFICITS AS AN ISSUE

To say that Walter Mondale and his advisors made the decision to make deficits the central issue of the 1984 campaign is a fact, but it is a fact that is somewhat misleading. In 1984, there was no significant segment of the elite opinion stream that did not believe that the large federal deficits of the Reagan years were the central public evil of those years. This included elites that were liberal and elites that were conservative—even elites that were sympathetic to Reagan and, on balance, favored his re-election despite what they saw as his failure on the deficit. Given that the Democrats nominated a candidate who had close ties and great affinity with the elite opinion stream, it would have been surprising if Mondale had decided to pick some other subject as the central theme of his campaign.

The popular opinion stream also saw federal deficits as an important evil, and thus as a valid issue. Given the preoccupation of the highly articulate elite opinion stream with the issue, and given the size of the Reagan deficits, this is no more surprising than the decision of the Mondale campaign to highlight it.

What apparently did surprise Democratic elites was that public opinion, as measured in polling, consistently and by increasing margins as the election year progressed, believed that Ronald Reagan and the Republican party were better able to handle the issue of deficits than Walter Mondale and the Democratic party. Deficits were portrayed by the elite opinion stream and by Mondale as an economic issue. The most threatening economic issue public opinion remembered was stagflation. Reagan had provided an answer to that issue: there was no stagflation in 1984. Public opinion decided that Reagan would be best suited to handle the most discussed economic issue of 1984, federal deficits.

It is conceivable that if he had provided public opinion with a persuasive answer to the issue of deficits, Mondale could have scored gains (if not won the election) on this issue. But his main answer was a large federal tax increase, and from the time he proposed it his tax program came under attack by the Reagan campaign and the Republican party. The Republicans (to the extent they offered any answer at all) emphasized that the answer to the deficit lay in domestic budget reduction and continued economic growth. Their main point was that, while they agreed that federal deficits were a public evil and thus an issue, Mondale's answer was the wrong answer. By overwhelming margins in every poll taken, public opinion agreed.

Even if public opinion had decided Mondale's answer to deficits was superior to Reagan's, it would not guarantee that the economic issue would have been a net plus for the Democrats in 1984. While regarded as a clear public evil, federal deficits could not match, in direct impact on the popular opinion stream, the 12–13 percent inflation and 20–21 percent interest rates during the latter part of Carter's term. And, in a sense, high taxes themselves could be depicted as a public evil even greater (and more painful) than the admitted public evil of the deficit. Reagan was not shy about making this argument in either 1980 or 1984.

Mondale's decision to call into question Reagan's handling of the economy, via the deficit issue, was a disaster for himself and his campaign. But it was not a blunder, because—like Henry Clay's decision in 1832 to shepherd through Congress a bank rechartering bill he knew Andrew Jackson would veto and campaign on—it was due to strong conviction rooted in a wide gulf between the popular and elite opinion streams. The extent of this gulf was highlighted by the fact that the nation's most elite congressional district, the "Silk Stocking" Fifteenth District of Manhattan's East Side, was one of the very few in the nation in which Mondale in 1984 scored an enormous gain over Carter in 1980. Mondale won the district by 22 percent while losing the nation by 18; Carter had won the district by just 16 percent in a much closer 10-point national loss. Clearly, the 1981 tax cut was the Reagan program the elite opinion stream most disagreed with, and this conviction shaped the 1984 campaign.

PUBLIC OPINION AND ISSUE VOTING

Because of the numerical dominance of the popular opinion stream, public opinion is oriented toward issues—which usually means combatting public evils—rather than personalities. The larger the public evil is, the more issue voting there is. An incumbent administration that fails to provide an answer to a valence issue—that is, a public evil widely acknowledged as such—is certain to grow in unpopularity. As every politician knows, in assessing the strength of incumbent political elites at any time in any democracy, the first questions to ask are: is something widely perceived as very bad happening in the country—a depression, a collapse of standards, extreme vulnerability to enemy invasion? And, if so, what answers are the incumbent elites offering? If a response to these questions is fairly clear, it tells a great deal about that country's present politics, even before any question need be asked about the date of the next election or the answers of the probable opposition. The reason this test works is that the popular opinion stream is issue-oriented, and can seldom afford to be anything else.

If the opposite were true, if the popular opinion stream were personality-oriented rather than issue-oriented, then popular *control* over issues would make no dent in personality voting. That is, even though the electorate had ultimate command of the agenda and resolution of issues, politics would be just as likely to revolve around personalities as in countries where these elected personalities have a monopoly in dealing with issues.

The one country where the electorate has such ultimate control over issues is the one country that has virtually no personality in its politics. The presidency of Switzerland is rotated each year among the members of a seven-person council; incumbent national officeholders are little known and rarely defeated; the issue part of direct democracy, initiative and referendum, is frequently used, but recall of officeholders almost never; politics is calm, party balance changes glacially, and turnout for parliamentary elections is often low. The governing elites, if they can be called that, are

domesticated to the idea of popular control, and they rarely inter-
pret defeat in a referendum they have proposed as a vote of no
confidence in the government, according to Margaret Canovan in
her 1981 historical study, *Populism*.

When judging incumbent political elites, the popular opinion
stream is both results-oriented and future-oriented. It cares about
the present and the past primarily because this experience is its
best guide to the future. If the present trend of things under the
present incumbents is favorable—if community standards are being maintained and public evils, if they exist, are either manageable
or in visible decline—public opinion is likely to have a favorable
view of the incumbents. As Michael Barone has pointed out, one of
the clearest early portents for Reagan's re-election occurred when
polls asking voters whether things were headed in the right direction took a positive turn in the middle of Reagan's first term—the
first time this had happened since the Kennedy administration.

Public opinion judges the record of incumbent elites not with an
eye toward awarding merit badges or demerits, but as a forecast of
how things are likely to go in the future. This was underlined in
1978 in California when Governor Jerry Brown strongly opposed
Proposition 13 and saw his favorable rating drop. When the tax-
cutting initiative passed in the June primary, Brown immediately
accepted the results and took visible, tangible steps to implement
the new statute. His popularity went back up and he was easily re-
elected in November against a Republican opponent who had supported Proposition 13 all along. The popular opinion stream will
adjust its view of a political leader if his policies change to its
satisfaction: it is less interested in motive than probable future
result. Brown's re-election also confirms the Swiss experience that
in a situation where the electorate exercises ultimate control of
policy, it has little interest in punishing incumbent elites—
provided those elites show suitable submission to the verdict of
public opinion.

The conclusion of V. O. Key in *The Responsible Electorate*, his
study of presidential voting at a time when straight-ticket partisan
voting was much more prevalent than now, is pertinent: "From our

analyses the voter emerges as a *person* who appraises the actions of government, who has policy preferences, and who relates his vote to those appraisals and preferences. One may have misgivings about the data and one can certainly concede that the data also indicate that some voters are governed by blind party loyalty and that some others respond automatically to the winds of the environment of the moment. Yet the obtrusive feature of the data is the large number of persons whose vote is instrumental to their policy preferences."[29]

ORIGIN OF ISSUES

Although the popular opinion stream is the more issue-oriented part of public opinion once an issue is established, at most times it depends on the elite opinion stream to establish the issue in the first place. The creation of an issue initially requires (at times other than foundings, revolutions, and constitution-writing) the identification of a social condition by someone as a public evil. For the condition to become an issue, at least a significant segment of public opinion must agree that the social condition is in fact a public evil. Expertise and articulateness help in winning over such a segment to this view, and these qualities are a near-monopoly of the elite opinion stream.

Four books published in the 1960s provide examples of the creation of issues, initially by identification of a condition as a public evil, later by their acceptance as such by at least a large share of public opinion. The books, together with the issues they were influential in creating, were: Rachel Carson, *Silent Spring*, the issue of pesticide overkill; Ralph Nader, *Unsafe at Any Speed*, the issue of inadequate auto safety; Betty Friedan, *The Feminine Mystique*, the issue of female stereotyping; and Michael Harrington, *The Other America*, the issue of widespread poverty in an affluent society. All of these books were important not only in creating new issues, but as factors giving rise to political movements to counter the public evils they described: environmentalism, auto safety regulation, feminism, and the War on Poverty. All these movements existed in one form or another in earlier periods, but they received either revival or strong new momentum from these four books.

In periods when there is a gulf between the elite and popular opinion streams, and particularly when that gulf is along populist-elitist lines as has been the case since the 1960s, issues are more likely to originate in the popular opinion stream. An example was the issue of the ongoing negotiations to cede the Panama Canal to Panama in the 1960s and 1970s.

These negotiations, which began under President Johnson, at first attracted little or no opposition in the elite opinion stream, even among military and conservative elites which might have been expected to object strongly. After completing his second term as governor of California in January 1975, however, Ronald Reagan embarked on a speaking tour in which, in a "throwaway" line of his standard political speech, he cited the Panama Canal negotiations as a symptom of America's decline in the world. The responses were explosive, and Reagan gradually expanded on the issue. In 1976, he revived his flagging primary challenge to President Ford in part by highlighting the Panama Canal issue in a series of Southern primaries. By 1978, after the Panama Canal treaty had been ratified in the Senate, polling showed it to be a high-profile issue and a strong political negative for President Carter and those senators who had voted for it. A number of these senators were unexpectedly defeated in 1978 and 1980 by challengers who kept the issue alive.

From beginning to end, the Panama Canal issue saw a huge gulf in opinion between the popular and elite opinion streams. The popular opinion stream opposed the treaty and the elite opinion stream, including many articulate conservatives and anti-communists, supported it. The wave of popular revulsion to the treaty, whether regarded as old-fashioned jingoism of the worst sort or as a kind of proxy for a cluster of legitimate foreign-policy concerns, was an episode highly frustrating and unpleasant for both opinion streams. Reagan's eager use of the issue to win votes, often against the advice of his own aides, was for much of the elite opinion stream irrefutable proof that Reagan was a demagogue. His advocacy of a deep tax cut for individuals—another issue that had at least a partial origin in the popular opinion stream, via elite-opposed Proposition 13 in California—was still further proof of his demagogy. With their pessimism about the ability of people to respond to incentives, elitists tend to attribute advocacy of deep tax cuts to pandering to the electorate, rather than to a sincere belief in broad-based tax reduction as an answer to economic stagnation.

Reagan's frequent championing of ideas overwhelmingly opposed by the elites of his day would have been enough to foster tension between him and the elite opinion stream. A purely biographical factor which greatly accentuated this tension was Reagan's back-ground as an actor. This background, coupled with his willingness to delegate detail work to others, increased the tendency of elites, above all political elites, to regard Reagan as superficial and thus to underrate his ability.

In fact, in its elevation of candidates, the popular opinion stream frequently goes outside of trained political elites when public evils appear to be mounting. The unspoken assumption seems to be: if this is the best the politicians can do, let's try someone from outside politics. Very often, that someone has been a general: Washington was seen as a figure clearly apart from the squabbling state-level political elites in the chaotic period of the Articles of Confederation; Jackson was a clear, popular alternative to the establishmentarian, inbred political elites who dominated the Era of Good Feeling. Grover Cleveland, a local Buffalo lawyer, had never held office before 1881, but was catapulted to the presidency on his anti-corruption platform in 1884. Woodrow Wilson, a college president, had never run for office until 1910, but in 1912 was elected president as the embodiment of Progres-sive politics and the emerging populist democracy of direct voting. Such figures from outside politics as Grant and Eisenhower, like Washington, had little or no populist belief, but were still seen by popular opinion as refreshing alternatives to the ruling political elites they displaced.

In countries where political elites have a monopoly of candidate selection, it is more difficult for popular opinion to work its will at times when the popular and elite opinion streams are in conflict. In centralized parliamentary systems, popular opinion depends on the emergence of new elites from a self-perpetuating, hierarchical selection system, which is possible but unusual, or for emergence of a new party, which is cumbersome. No democracy is immune from troubling issues or even from crises, but a democracy that provides an outlet to the more issue-oriented part of public opinion, the popular opinion stream, is more likely to find itself regaining its equilibrium and finding answers to issues before crisis arrives.

CHAPTER 9

REALIGNMENT

REALIGNMENT is democracy's version of revolution. It is fascinating to elites, who sometimes describe it as if it were a simple substitution of one political elite at the top of society for another. But it is hard to find a realignment involving candidates but not issues or ideas. If it were merely a change of leadership and nothing more, a realignment could be declared and analyzed every time a powerful office changed hands, say by death or resignation of the president of the United States and his succession by the vice president. That such an event is clearly not in itself a realignment (however much it might contribute to one) suggests that realignment by definition has ideological content, and that the ideological change in question must have some staying power. In democracy, an ideological change that becomes a lasting part of the political landscape must have roots in public opinion.

ISSUE CLUSTERS

A shift in public opinion that leads to a realignment always involves one or more issues or (more likely) issue clusters. An issue cluster is a set of issues (public evils) that are related to each other in the view of public opinion.

In the previous chapter, stagflation was analyzed as a valence issue of the 1970s and early 1980s. The invention of the word stagflation made it possible to analyze it as if it were a single big issue, but like most big issues it can just as easily be analyzed as an issue cluster. The public evils of high inflation and low growth combined into an economic issue cluster. An additional public evil (certainly in the view of the popular opinion stream) was the related phenomenon of bracket creep, in which the combination of high inflation and stagnant growth in real incomes thrust most of the popular opinion stream into much higher marginal tax brackets, thus reducing their incomes by far more than stagnation by itself would have done. This made the tax-cut component of Reagan's answer to the economic issue more attractive and cogent to the popular opinion stream, since it could be regarded in part as an attempt to redress the mounting public evil of the bracket creep that affected most people, rather than as a radical, revolutionary proposal. Similarly, the multibillion-dollar surplus that built up in California's treasury between 1975 and 1978, ordinarily a social fact that might be regarded as a public good, added fuel to the view of California's popular opinion stream that the state's increased property tax burden for homeowners (mostly through upward assessment) was a clearly unnecessary public evil that needed the redress of Proposition 13.

Slavery can also be seen as a single public evil, predominantly a values issue between the North and South, that led to the election of Abraham Lincoln and to the Civil War. But this issue manifested itself, at various times and to different segments of public opinion, as a closely related succession or cluster of public evils. The Wilmot Proviso, first offered by an anti-slavery House Democrat and embraced by the Whigs at the time of the Mexican War, seemed a public evil to the South, since if enacted it would have excluded slavery from the vast new territories then being conquered. Later, the Fugitive Slave Law, which permitted Southern slaveholders to track runaway slaves into the heart of Northern states, made slavery a much more visible public evil to the North and at the same time seemed a kind of invasion of the Northern way of life. Still later, the Supreme Court's *Dred Scott* decision seemed to deny the national community any right to set its own standards concerning slavery, thus setting up a classic argument between social elitism and social populism. All during the generation before the Civil War, large segments of public opinion in both the North and the South saw as an overriding public evil the threat of disunion slavery represented, and one attempted answer to this issue was the Compromise of 1850.

As this example suggests, an issue cluster can persist as a multi-level argument in public opinion for many years, even generations. Ireland was a persistent issue cluster in British politics from the 1820s to the 1920s, and has become one again today. An issue cluster does not necessarily lead to political upheaval, but it can remain a major defining element between political parties and belief systems until it is resolved.

When an issue cluster gains in importance, it can lead to a party realignment, as was the case with slavery in 1860 and economic issue clusters in 1896 and 1932. Often, a political party becomes identified with an approach to an issue cluster that persists through realignment and counter-realignment. From Thomas Jefferson through Jimmy Carter, the Democratic party was always the party of internationalism in economics. Whenever the issue of free trade arose, the Democrats were predictably for lower tariffs and fewer trade restrictions than were their opponents—the Federalists, the Whigs, and the Republicans—until Walter Mondale's leaning toward protectionism broke this pattern in 1984.

Similarly, the Republicans have maintained the identity of the Whigs and Federalists as the party least sympathetic to foreign immigration. And, beginning with their successful effort to block the League of Nations, the Republicans maintained an isolationist stance until 1940, when a consciously internationalist wing led by Wendell Willkie won a pitched battle at the party's national convention and permanently reversed this position.

A favorable realignment clearly puts a party in a position to implement its answers to an issue cluster. But decisive success is often delayed. The Jacksonians won national elections on the economic issue cluster in 1832 and 1836, but the Whig victory of 1840 put their policy victories in doubt. Tariffs were raised, public works expanded, President Van Buren's Independent Treasury plan repealed, and the only thing that stopped the chartering of the Third Bank of the United States was the death of President Harrison and the succession of John Tyler, who disliked the Whig congressional leader, Henry Clay. Tyler vetoed two bank charter bills, and was read out of the party by the Whigs in Congress.

The Democrats won the election of 1844 over Clay by only a narrow margin, and the prominent issue was annexation of Texas rather than the economic issues that had dominated the previous several elections. But the fact that the Democrats had won as the party of continental expansion did not prevent President Polk, a dedicated Jacksonian, from decisively implementing his party's economic program as well. The economic issue may not have been uppermost in the mind of public opinion in 1844, but earlier battles had provided a clear identity on this issue cluster for both the Democrats and Whigs, and public opinion was in no doubt of the economic implications of a Jacksonian victory on such issues as central banking, tariffs, and the Whigs' American System of Federal-financed public works. Indeed, much of public opinion's partisan allegiance had formed on these issues, and such allegiances shape elections in tandem with more currently visible issues.

On the other hand, some important issue clusters are resolved without a realignment or even without clear party identification with the two sides of the issue in question. The civil rights revolution of the 1950s and 1960s saw a bipartisan moderate-to-liberal coalition prevail over conservatives of both parties. The concept of unilateral ("no fault") divorce laws was widely enacted at the state level in the 1960s and 1970s with little or no partisan or even ideological battling. Changes of these kinds are most likely to occur when a realignment of the elite opinion stream takes place that either leads the popular opinion stream toward a similar realignment or leaves it inert. The popular opinion stream is most likely to remain inert when an elite realignment is so complete that articulate opposition to the policy change is missing. The realignment on the civil rights issue was massive, but it had opposition, and a comparable debate and realignment took place in popular opinion. The revolution in divorce laws had virtually no elite opposition, and was translated into policy with little or no debate or controversy in public opinion as a whole.

ALTERNATION OF ISSUE CLUSTERS

In the last chapter, it was noted that while finding an answer to an issue is an important plus for a political leader or party, it does not assure that leader or party success in whatever issue succeeds it. This rule applies at least as strongly to issue clusters. With its orientation to issues and to the future, the popular opinion stream will quickly turn on an incumbent political elite if it shows inability to grapple with an emerging issue cluster, however successful this elite may have been in dealing with the dominant issue cluster of the earlier period. That is why the Republicans were wise to play down the economic issue in 1968, and why the Democrats were unwise to highlight the economic issue in 1984.

These recent examples have analogies throughout the history of mass democracy. Indeed, when answers are found, or appear to be found, to a cluster of valence issues, such as depression, stagflation, or a survival-threatening war, public opinion often turns its attention toward values issues.*

Why is this so? Why is public opinion not content with a strong economic recovery, or with victory in a war that seemed at the time

---

* Keeping in mind that realignment is the democratic version of revolution, it stands to reason that a sudden transition from valence to values issues in a non-democratic setting can lead to revolution. In *The Old Regime and the French Revolution*, Tocqueville outlines the successful achievement of economic growth by the government of Louis XVI, but goes on to add: "It is a singular fact that this steadily increasing prosperity, far from tranquilizing the population, everywhere promoted a spirit of unrest. The general public became more and more hostile to every ancient institution, more and more discontented; indeed, it was increasingly obvious that the nation was heading for a revolution."

a peril to national existence? Why, for example, was Winston Churchill not rewarded with a handsome victory by British public opinion in 1945, in gratitude for his incontestable contribution to national survival in World War II?

Part of the answer has already been mentioned. Public opinion is interested in past successes mainly as they relate to future challenges. However impressive the past accomplishments, if they appear unrelated to the issues immediately ahead, they will not necessarily be a plus in an election fought out on those new issues.

Perhaps even more important, at least according to the classical view of politics outlined in Chapter 3, the heart of politics is bound up in the setting of community standards. No one, least of all members of the popular opinion stream, would deny the importance of community survival, or of the ability of the bulk of the people to maintain economic well-being. But these are in a sense starting points for community life. People want to live, and people want to be allowed to produce enough to live, but if classical political thought is right people form and sustain a community for a purpose, to choose the agreed-on standards that constitute a way of life.

The elevation of George Washington to the presidency— uncontested—in 1789 successfully launched the federal union, but even before he left office values issues related to political equality had put his party under siege and were soon to extinguish it as a national force. The triumph of the Jacksonian economic and military agenda under President Polk led to a staggering expansion of both the American economy and physical territory. Yet by 1860 the national Democratic party carried only twelve of a possible 303 votes in the Electoral College and was reduced to a seventy-two-

---

Tocqueville notes that revolutionary sentiment was most evident not in sectors left behind by economic growth, but in "those parts of France in which the improvement in the standard of living was most pronounced." This corresponds to recent democratic experience, in which the most economically affluent classes of students led campus revolts in the United States, France, and elsewhere in the 1960s, and in the succeeding period in which economic boom areas of the South and West showed the greatest sentiment for pro-Republican presidential realignment. [30]

year-long minority status, because it was unable to deal with the values issue of slavery in the midst of the economic boom of the 1850s.

More recently, the political elite that achieved a revolution in France in 1958 succeeded, under Charles de Gaulle, in: stabilizing politics through the electoral reforms mentioned in Chapter 8; ending inflation, cutting taxes, and generating an economic boom via the economic reforms centered on creation of the New Franc; and ending the draining Algerian War with the overwhelming support of public opinion as ratified in a government-sponsored referendum. Yet by the end of the 1960s, de Gaulle had been forced out of office not by economics or war, but by a values crisis that brought his nation to a virtual standstill in June 1968. It did not cause a party realignment because his premier and successor, Georges Pompidou, was able to tap the forces of counterrevolution as well as the popular opinion stream's basic trust in the Gaullists' remarkable domestic achievements. But these achievements had little relevance for de Gaulle's own survival, once the popular opinion stream concluded he was baffled by the cultural crisis of the late 1960s.

In a parallel development, American Democrats were highly successful in dealing with the economic issue in the 1960s, but not so successful in achieving mastery of the transition from valence issues to the values issues that coincided with the resumption of strong growth.

The resolution of valence issues, even the finding of clear answers to these issues, may achieve peace and prosperity and win political elites a place of honor in history books. But if those same elites fail to understand the values issue cluster that so often follows, realignment toward new answers and new elites will quickly occur. This happens due to the overconfidence that is natural to successful elites, but also because values issue clusters are significantly different from valence issue clusters, and the talents needed to deal with one are not identical with those needed to deal with the other.

NEW DEAL REALIGNMENT

In Chapter 8, the proposed ratification of the Panama Canal treaty was discussed as an example of an issue that evoked opposite reactions from the popular and elite opinion streams. Although the answer of the elite opinion stream prevailed with Senate ratification of the treaty in 1978, polls found it to be a factor in the defeat of a number of Democratic senators in 1978 and 1980, which in turn helped Republicans take over the Senate for the first time in twenty-six years. In other words, opposite reactions to an issue by the two opinion streams contributed to a significant change in the composition of the nation's political elite.

When such a split between the two opinion streams occurs not merely on an issue, but on an issue cluster that has achieved dominance in a nation's political debate, the result is often a partisan realignment. When the popular opinion stream develops a strong view on an issue cluster it sees as central and urgent, and finds incumbent political elites not only not responsive to this view, but moving in precisely the opposite direction, it is extremely likely to remove incumbent elites (assuming a viable set of challenger elites exists) at the earliest opportunity. Such a change is likely to prove long-lasting if the challenger elites provide an answer to the issue once in office. If it sees these answers to the issue cluster as successful, the popular opinion stream is unlikely soon to trust the displaced elites to carry out a mandate on future issues, particularly related ones.

These natural tendencies are made even sharper if the divergent answers to the issue cluster have a significant populist-elitist component. All these elements were present in the 1930s, when in the Depression the Republicans, and particularly Herbert Hoover, resisted aiding people and instead supported extensive aid for elite-controlled institutions such as large corporations. Influenced by nascent Keynesian theories of demand stimulus, the Democrats leaned more to direct aid to people as the most effective form of government relief. Whether or not it was more effective economically, its implicit populism helped make it more effective politically.

If the Republicans had quickly retreated from Hooverism after 1932, they might possibly have re-established their seventy-two-year-old dominance in 1936, particularly given the Democrats' failure to end the Depression. But elite opinion trended against the New Deal approach rather than for it; in fact, Roosevelt became a "traitor to his class" for many members of the American elite. Alfred Landon, the Republican nominee in 1936, was militantly anti-New Deal and did significantly better in newspaper endorsements than Hoover had done in 1932.

Even more strikingly, the *Literary Digest*, then the pre-eminent magazine of American elites, conducted a poll that found its elite-leaning sample of telephone and car owners strongly for Landon, providing a reverse image of the trend of popular opinion. In 1932, the *Literary Digest* poll had been strongly for Roosevelt, mirroring the results in popular opinion and suggesting that between 1932 and 1936, the two opinion streams were moving in opposite directions.

The Roosevelt years were dominated by the valence issues of depression and world war. By the 1940s, it was evident that the Democrats under Roosevelt and Truman were providing answers to these issues, and the split between the two opinion streams lost much of the virulence of 1936. But it was still there. In 1948, Republican Governor Thomas Dewey of New York was overwhelmingly the candidate of the elite opinion stream, which is in part why his victory was widely written about as inevitable even after his Gallup Poll lead had dwindled to 5 percent in October. The Republican share of the vote in 1948 was steadily higher the greater the voters' education and income. In 1948 it was taken for granted that elites tended to be considerably more conservative than average voters on the major domestic issues of the day. Dewey carried almost all of the Eastern states, which throughout American history have been the states most influenced by the elite opinion stream. He lost almost everywhere else.

COMMUNISM AND THE OPINION STREAMS

In the late 1940s and early 1950s, an important issue cluster that could be summed up under the name "communism" arose. Like the New Deal issue cluster, it had decidedly different impacts on the two opinion streams, but its overall impact caused a convergence of elite and popular opinion that could be seen as correcting the 1930s' divergence.

In part, the issue cluster of communism was a continuation of the debate over intervention that had divided the New Deal alignment along ethnic lines prior to Pearl Harbor. Irish, Italian, and German voters were strongly Democratic in 1932 and 1936, but their views on foreign policy made them skeptical of Roosevelt's pro-intervention policy, and Republicans scored gains among these voters even though their isolationist wing was defeated at the 1940 convention. Many of these same anti-interventionist voters were more likely than typical Democrats to adopt anti-communist views in the late 1940s and early 1950s.

There were some cross-cutting movements in the popular opinion stream, but on balance the communist issue cluster made the electorate more Republican in the 1950s.

The reverse was true of the elite opinion stream, particularly when the issue of communism spread into the domestic arena in the form of the internal security issue. In particular, the anti-communist investigations of Senator Joseph McCarthy, which passionately divided the popular opinion stream, were overwhelmingly opposed by the elite opinion stream, driving many elite voters toward more liberal and Democratic alignments.

The Republicans scored gains in 1950 and won the presidency and Congress in 1952 on the slogan "communism, corruption, and Korea," and were able to halt the fighting in Korea within months of Dwight Eisenhower's election. But the communist issue cluster failed as a realignment issue. The Democrats deflected it by making sure it was seen as a valence issue—which methods were appropriate to stop the acknowledged public evil of communism? By the 1960 election it was hard to say whether Kennedy or Nixon was more militantly anti-communist. Nixon had been a firmer anti-communist on the internal-security or domestic part of the issue (though liberals criticized Kennedy for his failure to condemn McCarthy), but in foreign and defense policy Kennedy seemed the more militant, with his attacks on the missile gap and his Wilsonian commitment to intervene abroad on behalf of freedom.

The Republicans under Eisenhower received generally good marks for their conduct of foreign policy. But three recessions marred their economic record and, with the two parties' convergence on the issue cluster of communism, the Democrats were able to revive the economic issue cluster that had served them so well in the 1930s and 1940s. In 1958, the Democrats won their greatest congressional majorities in two decades, and in 1960 they narrowly regained the presidency on the pro-growth slogan, "Let's get this country moving again."

CHAPTER 10

THE RISE OF VALUES POLITICS, 1963–68

THE DEMOCRATS SUCCEEDED in fulfilling their pledge of stronger growth. The last Eisenhower recession ended early in 1961, and the next subsequent recession did not begin until late 1969—at nearly nine years, the longest expansion in American history. Yet in 1968, in the midst of continued growth, the Democrats lost the White House and have had trouble winning it ever since.

It is extremely difficult, even at more than two decades' remove, to sum up the political crosscurrents at work in the 1960s. A big reason is that many of that decade's battles are still alive in today's politics. Partisan power has changed little from the pattern that emerged in the national election of 1968: Republican predominance at the presidential level, a Democratic edge in Congress and in most states. In this sense, the story of the 1960s is still going on.

Yet, at least in retrospect, one statement can clearly be made about the central issues of 1960s politics: they were all, at bottom, values issues. As the 1960s wore on, the big valence issues that had dominated the three previous decades—depression and world war; at first how to emerge from them, later on how to avoid a repetition of them—either disappeared or greatly receded.

They did so in large part because of Democratic successes. However much Republicans argued about the true causes, the Depression *did* end under Roosevelt. In the prosperous generation that followed World War II, Democrats Truman, Kennedy, and Johnson suffered just one recession in sixteen years, Republican Eisenhower three in eight years. World War II *was* won under Roosevelt. The two parties could share credit for avoiding World War III, but it was under a Democrat, President Kennedy, that the Cuban missile crisis was interpreted worldwide as an American victory that greatly lessened the fear of nuclear war as a central issue in global politics. From 1963 on, with the record-breaking expansion solidly under way and no recurrence of a Cuba- or Berlin-style confrontation with the Soviet Union, the valence issues of nuclear peace and economic growth faded gradually from the scene, except as loudly proclaimed Democratic achievements that argued against the thought of Republican restoration.

The trigger for the politics of values that was to mark the 1960s was the drive for black civil rights. As noted in the last chapter, passage of the civil rights bills of 1964 and 1965 turned out to be bipartisan and did not, of itself, pose a serious threat of realignment. It is true that five Deep South states voted for Republican nominee Barry Goldwater in 1964, in large part because of his opposition to the 1964 bill. But Goldwater received fewer electoral votes in the South as a whole than had Eisenhower in 1952 or 1956, and he was crushed in every other region of the country. Following that election, it appeared that Kennedy and his successor, Lyndon Johnson, had deftly reversed their party's long-standing poor performance on civil rights and put Democratic presidential politics on a firmer footing than ever.

But the drive for black equality proved to be much more a beginning of conflict than an end. It helped fuel an astonishing wave of social unrest and re-evaluation that spread into every corner of 1960s American culture.

—Between 1963 and 1968, black rioting occurred in virtually every American city, displacing in prominence the civil rights demonstrations of the late 1950s and early 1960s. The riots that followed the passage of the landmark Civil Rights Act of 1964 were far more severe than those preceding it.

—Between 1964 and 1970, a wave of student unrest swept through America's college campuses, which in their entire previous history had been peaceful. The coincidence of this wave of unrest with black rioting, with a slight lag, suggests that the issue of black equality may have been a necessary precursor of campus unrest. This is underlined by the fact that Mario Savio, the leader of the first campus revolt—the Berkeley Free Speech Movement of 1964—was a veteran of civil rights crusades in the South.

—With the dispatch of American combat troops in 1965, the Vietnam War became a society-splitting values issue that seemed to pit generations and social classes against each other in a way that bore no resemblance to the debate over a similar limited war in Korea a decade and a half earlier.

Important as it was in turning a values conflict into a values crisis, the Vietnam War had virtually no role in pre-1965 black or campus unrest. Little or no mention of the war is to be found, for example, in accounts of the Berkeley uprising. This suggests that the nature of the Vietnam debate stemmed from a values conflict already going on—in contrast to the commonly held assumption that U.S. intervention in Vietnam was itself the trigger for an American values conflict. Almost from the beginning of American combat intervention in Vietnam, and in stark contrast to Korea fifteen years earlier, much of the debate was about the morality, rather than the practicality, of U.S. intervention. Ultimately, in other words, the flash point of the debate was not: Can the United States make its values prevail in Vietnam, but: *Should* American values prevail in Vietnam—or, by implication, anywhere else?*

---

* In contrast to Vietnam, the Korean War issue in American politics was overwhelmingly a valence issue. This was true in two senses.

First, it was a debate about how to stop communism. No articulate element on either side argued that stopping communism in Korea was undesirable. One side (the Republicans) argued communism could be stopped and bloodshed lessened with a stronger show of force than favored by the leading Democrats, President Truman and Secretary of State Dean Acheson. Democrats, in reply, argued that overeager advocacy of force by such figures as the

VALUES CRISIS AMONG ELITES

At first glance there would seem to be little reason for a successful policy result—the civil rights revolution of the early 1960s—to lead to a values crisis that saw campus rioting, a virulent debate over a limited war in Asia, and, ultimately, a cultural upheaval best summed up in the word "counterculture." Why would passage of landmark civil rights bills in 1964 and 1965, apparently resolving the unfinished business of the Civil War, not lead instead to increased self-confidence among elites, particularly the Democratic elites in large measure responsible?

First, the drive for black equality coincided with new attention among elites to the issue of equality in general. Were there other groups in American society that had failed to be accorded their rightful equality? What about Hispanics, American Indians, women? What was the nature of equality itself? Could blacks take advantage of their newly won civil equality to make similar advances in the economic arena? Or was the cultural gap between white and black America too great for this to be a realistic hope? Did black rioting in the midst of civil rights successes suggest that these successes were more apparent than real; that the problem was much deeper, more fundamental? How much "equality" could there be in a society that set records for national wealth and yet still contained tens of millions of people, white and black, in a culture of poverty?

The answers given to these questions by American elites, particularly intellectual and campus elites, became more and more pessimistic as the decade of the 1960s wore on. Political equality—

American commander, General Douglas MacArthur, risked nuclear war with Russia.

Both points of contention—the stopping of communism in Asia and the avoidance of nuclear war with Russia—were valence issues in the period of the Korean debate (1950–53). Significant isolationist sentiment existed in the popular opinion stream, as it has in virtually all periods of American history, but it played a surprisingly small role in the debate led by policy elites. The Taft wing of the GOP, which by and large had opposed creation of NATO, was militantly hawkish on the spread of Asian communism and tended to be strongly behind MacArthur in the Korean War policy debate.

one man, one vote—came to seem increasingly peripheral, even meaningless, when compared to the deeply embedded flaws of American culture as a whole.

The special situation of American campuses in the mid–1960s created a particularly explosive milieu during the years President Johnson escalated American involvement in Vietnam. Undergraduates, for one thing, had an automatic deferment from the military draft. After graduation they had the option of extending their deferment by going into certain types of graduate training, or into teaching. Given the overall mood of rising social concern, this privilege made students far more likely than otherwise to oppose the war, and to oppose it on moral rather than practical grounds. In the age of civil rights, the clear violation of civil equality involved in the student deferment made society as a whole seem corrupt to many students.

In the post-World War II period, moreover, the university population had grown enormously in numbers and status. Such factors as the G.I. Bill, the orientation toward children signified by the baby boom, and Soviet space successes in the 1950s had combined to make college education a national priority and a college degree a prized precondition of entry into elite status. States such as California built vast university systems almost from scratch in the decades after World War II. It was on the campus of the pre-eminent school in California's state system, the University of California at Berkeley, that the first major unrest erupted in 1964.

In these boom years for universities, it is hardly surprising that intellectuals enjoyed a vast rise in status. From the ineffectual "egghead" stereotype of the 1940s and 1950s, to the hip Harvard reformers of the Kennedy years, to the arbiters of culture (Norman Mailer, James Baldwin) of the later 1960s was a swift ascent—to the point where a decision by the poet Robert Lowell, in 1965, to turn down an invitation to the White House was seen, at the time and subsequently, as a major breakthrough in domestic opposition to the Vietnam War.

Paradoxically, many of the intellectuals who were gaining status in the 1960s had come of age in an era when the situation was very different—the late 1940s and early 1950s. That time of anti-communist investigations and legislation made the careers of such figures as Richard Nixon and Joseph McCarthy, neither of them noted for his positive views of American intellectuals. The popular backing gained by critics of intellectuals made a deep impression on American intellectual elites, one that by no means dissipated after the loyalty investigations wound down following McCarthy's censure by the Senate in 1954.

Well before the upheavals of the mid-1960s, a much darker view gained ground among intellectuals and professors, not just of the typical voter, but at times about the key premises of American democracy itself. A particularly influential book among historians was Richard Hofstadter's *The Age of Reform* (1955), which characterized such movements as Populism and Progressivism as episodes involving the mass acting out of negative feelings, rather than as straightforward attempts to reform society. More radical critiques of American democracy, including the "revisionist" school which blamed the Democratic administrations of the 1940s for the Cold War, as well as outright Marxist class analysis, also gained influence, particularly on campus. This growing intellectual alienation provided a key backdrop to the events of the 1960s.

The election of John Kennedy, with his Harvard aura and choice of academics for a number of key policy positions in his administration, gave intellectuals as much pure political status as they have enjoyed at any time in American history. This only made their disillusionment more intense following the series of political shocks that defined the first half of the 1960s: the Kennedy assassination of 1963, the beginning of black and campus rioting in 1963–64, and the introduction of American combat troops into Vietnam in 1965. By 1966, the hopes of the Kennedy years seemed distant or unimportant to most intellectuals. Intellectuals, professors, and their students on campuses all over America were concluding not only that society was corrupt, but that conventional politics offered little or no chance of fixing it.

One result, of course, was a swift rise in radical politics among intellectual elites, particularly the young. A movement that began as a student-led protest against educational bureaucrats on campus quickly escalated into a challenge to society as a whole. Part of the challenge, often called the New Left or the Movement, was overtly political. But a perhaps even more influential strain advocated the forsaking not just of conventional politics, but of conventional society itself. The rise of the counterculture, with its across-the-board rejection of society and its norms, was on the surface non-political, but in a profounder sense it was the ultimate manifestation of values politics. It had strong impact not just on its young adherents, but on the older generation. The special strength "the Movement" and the counterculture had on elite campuses ensured that the 1960s brought not just generational revolt, but a crisis of confidence in America's elite opinion stream as a whole.

Around 1967, the balance among powerful political and journalistic elites began to tip toward the views of society's harshest critics. One milestone was appointment of the Kerner Commission on urban rioting, which was to assign the blame for the riots to "white racism"—in effect, to American culture as a whole. Another was the announcement that same year by *Time* magazine of its opposition to the American role in Vietnam. *Time*, whose influence as the elites' leading mass-circulation magazine corresponded to that of the *Literary Digest* thirty years earlier, was noted for its hawkishness on Far Eastern affairs and for proclaiming the twentieth century as the "American Century." Its defection to the dovish cause was felt instantly not only in the world of journalism—the increasingly powerful television networks soon followed—but in the world of corporate and Republican elites.

In late 1967, Secretary of Defense Robert McNamara—the chief architect of the administration's war policy—privately concluded that the doves were right and resigned his office early the following year. President Johnson, still determined to press the war effort to a successful conclusion, selected as his successor Clark Clifford, an enormously respected pillar of the Washington establishment who as a White House aide had been a key advocate of President Truman's Cold War policy. Widely assumed to be a Vietnam hawk, Clifford began siding with the doves soon after taking office. No matter how hard he tried, the president could not seem to recruit new blood willing to help him combat the growing pessimism on Vietnam in his party and administration.

1968: WORLDWIDE VALUES CLASH

The year 1968 saw an assault on incumbent elites all over the world; in reach it far exceeded the year 1848 in which monarchies across Europe tottered. Civil unrest reached a significant level in countries as varied as the United States, Mexico, France, West Germany, Japan, China, and Czechoslovakia, to make just a partial listing. Even the most stable institution in human history, the Roman Catholic Church, saw an upsurge of vehement dissent following the July publication of Pope Paul's encyclical reaffirming a ban on artificial contraception.

As in the United States, many of these conflicts had their roots earlier in the 1960s, and many have not fully played themselves out even today. In the short run—and similarly to the widespread unrest of 1848—most of the institutions that came under attack survived. In China, the Cultural Revolution begun by Mao in 1965 concluded its violent phase while in Czechoslovakia the Soviet army restored the status quo. The Gaullists stayed in power in France, as did the Institutional Revolutionary party in Mexico along with most other long-ruling elites.

But in nearly every instance, the challenge was radical in nature and directed primarily at "the system," and only secondarily at specific local grievances. Coming at the end of a decade of the greatest global economic growth in history, 1968 represented a worldwide explosion of the values politics that had begun with the early–1960s civil rights revolution in the United States.

In the communist world, the elites under attack were old-style communist bureaucrats, but the attacks came from ideologically opposite directions. In China, party chairman Mao orchestrated a top-down campaign of intimidation and terror against virtually all elite institutions, pre-eminently the party. The major sin of the

Chinese elites seemed to be elite status itself: was such status consistent with the radical Marxist vision of equality of result? Mao and his allies tried to resolve this tension at the heart of Marxism-Leninism by such measures as abolition of ranks in the military and sending professors and scientists to the fields during harvest season to purge them of their lust for elite status.

In contrast, the communist elites in Czechoslovakia came under attack for ideological rigidity, not lassitude, and the assault was far more peaceful, at least until the Soviet invasion in June. The drive by party leader Alexander Dubcek to put incentives into economic life and openness into political life proved far more prophetic of future reform efforts in the communist world than did the Great Proletarian Cultural Revolution in China.

In the context of 1968, this hardly seemed likely. The Dubcek experiment was violently snuffed out and appeared to have few imitators, in Eastern Europe or elsewhere. And radical Maoism, though the violent phase of the Cultural Revolution peaked in 1968 and ended just afterward, remained firmly in power in China and won admirers throughout the intellectual population of the Western and Third Worlds.

In the non-communist world, the turmoil of 1968 had two common features: it had a heavy student/intellectual component and came from the political Left. But in a number of respects, the New Left of the 1960s had a different shape and feel from the Old Left of the 1930s and 1940s. Surprisingly for a movement whose leadership was drawn heavily from intellectuals and students with elite status, the New Left had tendencies that were both anti-elitist and anti-intellectual. Part of this strain was no doubt due to the widespread interest in Maoism in New Left circles. But, as James Billington pointed out in his study of revolution, *Fire in the Minds of Men*, much New Left theory bore a striking resemblance to the quasi-populist, anti-Marxist socialism preached in the first half of the nineteenth century by Pierre-Joseph Proudhon: "There was, first of all, the intense moralism and quasi-anarchic rejection of almost all established authority. There was the accompanying Proudhonian desire to put power directly in the hands of 'the

people,' primarily by the nonviolent strengthening of local commu-
nal structures. At the same time there was a deep antagonism to
dogma and 'idea-mania' as well as an indifference to history, and
suspicion of science. They followed Proudhon in protesting against
remote central power, and arguing for immediate concrete benefits
against the distant, symbolic goals promoted by governments."[31]

The Old Left of the 1930s had surged at a time of global depression, when capitalism seemed in danger of breaking down. Much of
its argument was for the higher *efficiency* of the socialist model, and
the hallmark of its vision of efficiency was confidence in central
economic planning by a cadre of political and technocratic elites. To
a considerable degree, the Old Left scored political gains in the
1930s and afterward by having a new and (at the time) plausible
answer to the valence issue of world depression. The doctrine of
central planning had great impact, leaving in its wake enormously
larger and more powerful centralized bureaucracies, even in nations that failed to adopt an overtly left-of-center agenda. In whatever incarnation, democratic or non-democratic, the Old Left
grappled primarily with valence issues and forwarded answers that
were overtly elitist.

By contrast, the New Left of the 1960s surged in a time of global
growth, which included strong growth in the newly independent
Third World. In this environment, few were attracted to radical
socialism as a superior growth model. Its appeal was its expression
of certain values, particularly personal fulfillment and equality of
condition, or some combination of the two. These values entailed,
at least by implication, suppression rather than elevation of economic, political, and other elites.

In fact, in country after country, a chief target of the New Left
proved to be the very bureaucracies that the ideas of the Old Left
had helped bring into being. The gulf between the "scientific
socialism" of the Old Left and a movement that thrived on such
slogans as "Power to the People" and "Don't Trust Anyone Over 30"
is obvious, and at least in part is explained by the fact that the New
Left arose in an era of values politics and its answers had a populist
or at least anti-elitist content.

Left populism—in the United States, France, and elsewhere—reached its zenith in 1968. In many if not most of the democratic countries that experienced turmoil that year, the reaction of the popular opinion stream was far from appreciative; even the Communist-voting blue-collar suburbs of Paris failed to respond to the student revolt that disrupted that city. In subsequent elections where the New Left revolt became an issue, such as the French national election of 1969, the popular opinion stream showed a marked conservative trend. As this lack of popular response became increasingly evident to New Left leaders, the populist tinge of 1960s leftism faded.

But the commitment of the New Left to a values revolution never did. If anything, with the failure of left populism, it deepened. Furthermore, the indifference of the popular opinion stream was not shared by the elite opinion stream. Just as in the United States, where the rise of the counterculture helped shake the commitment of elites to continuing the war in Vietnam, the challenge to traditional values found elite sympathy well outside the intellectual elite, the New Left's vanguard. In one striking example, during the civil unrest of 1968, Luis Echeverria, the justice minister, led the suppression of Mexico City rioting that shed the blood of hundreds of students; in 1970, he was elevated by the one-party Mexican state to the presidency at least partly as a reward for preserving the status quo. After taking office, Echeverria surprised many of his backers by shifting government policy sharply to the left at home and abroad.

As for the United States, the country furthest advanced along the road of 1960s values politics, 1968 proved to be the most violent year of its history since the Civil War, and the country has never been the same since.

1968: COLLAPSE OF LIBERAL POLICY

The year 1968 was experienced by Americans as a series of violent shocks beginning in January and peaking in August. In November, the nation narrowly replaced the Democrats with the Republicans in the White House—a victory that seemed aberrational to many at the time, but in fact inaugurated a Republican era in presidential politics that continues to the present.

The shocks were: the Tet offensive in Vietnam, which began in late January and ended in early February; the Eugene McCarthy primary showing in New Hampshire in March; the withdrawal of President Johnson from his race for re-election on the last day of March; the assassination of Dr. Martin Luther King, followed by a nationwide outbreak of black rioting, in April; the assassination of Robert Kennedy in June; and the rioting at the Democratic National Convention in Chicago in August.

To the extent that the 1960s can be summed up as a time of civil unrest that shook elite value systems to their roots, the Tet offensive was perfectly designed. Meticulously planned by North Vietnam's battle-hardened generals, it took the shape of simultaneous popular rebellion in hundreds of population centers throughout South Vietnam. By conventional accounting a military failure—almost all territorial gains were quickly reclaimed by American or South Vietnamese forces within days—the Tet offensive was seen all over the world, and particularly among elites in the United States, as a breakdown of American war policy in Indochina. The most indelible picture of the Tet offensive was not the protracted struggle for Hue, which took thousands of lives both military and civilian, but the communist occupation of part of the American embassy grounds in Saigon. These pictures, relayed worldwide by American network television, implied to many a collapse of the U.S. position not simply in Vietnam but throughout the world.

The impact of the Tet offensive inside the Johnson administration was explosive, even before much was known of its political implications for the upcoming primary season. On the surface, the administration made calm statements about the military situation, in particular the cost to the Vietcong infrastructure which led the assault in most places and suffered huge losses. Internally, the reaction was closer to panic. The American commander, General William Westmoreland, requested huge new deployments of American troops—more than 200,000—to be added to the half-million-plus already stationed in Vietnam. From the outset, the request was seen as politically suicidal—and as a tacit confession of strategic bankruptcy by those who made it. In particular, Secretary of Defense Clifford used the troop request to call into question American war policy as a whole.

In the middle of this review, on March 12, came the year's second big political shock: the first-in-the-nation New Hampshire primary. The anti-Vietnam war candidacy of Minnesota Senator Eugene McCarthy, underfunded and seemingly of minor importance, received 42 percent of the vote compared to Johnson's 49 percent write-in vote. McCarthy's campaign was aided by the impact of the Tet offensive, but even earlier it had generated an outpouring of support from college campuses from around the country (and particularly the elite colleges of the Northeast where the New Left was strongest). In the aftermath of the primary, New York Senator Robert Kennedy—former attorney general and brother of the slain president—entered the nomination fight against Johnson.

With these political developments as a backdrop, a kind of culmination in the administration's war review occurred on March 25. At the president's request, a council of "wise men" had been periodically meeting for several years to give advice about the war. The group included the cream of America's post-World War II diplomatic and military elite: former Secretary of State Dean Acheson, former National Security Advisor McGeorge Bundy, retired Generals Omar Bradley, Matthew Ridgeway, and Maxwell Taylor, to name a few. This group, with a single exception—former Under Secretary of State George Ball—had been supportive of the American commitment in Vietnam. But now, after a series of secret briefings, a majority of the group went over to the dovish side and so informed the president on Tuesday, March 26. Within two days, a major speech in successive drafts had changed its tenor from hawkish to dovish, and on Sunday, March 31, Johnson announced a partial bombing halt in North Vietnam and his own withdrawal from his race for re-election.

Certainly voter dissatisfaction was a key factor in the president's mind; the Wisconsin primary, in which he was certain to lose to

McCarthy, was just two days away. But in 1968, the nominating process was much less voter-centered than it became in 1972 and afterward. There is very little doubt that Johnson could have bulldozed his way to renomination; the eventual nominee, Vice President Hubert Humphrey, won as Johnson's handpicked successor without winning, or even entering, a single primary. But whatever Johnson's true motivation for withdrawal—extensive preparations for his re-election were taking place well after New Hampshire and well after his probable defeat in Wisconsin had become known—the turning of the elite group of "wise men" visibly shook his determination to continue. The cracking of the elite opinion stream, which had begun to be clearly evident the year before, had reached the topmost levels, including two secretaries of defense and the surviving architects of the postwar anticommunist policy of containment. In this context, it is no wonder the president felt obliged to reverse his policy and end his presidency.

The race for the Democratic nomination was transformed by Tet, New Hampshire, and the Johnson reversal/withdrawal. It was now fundamentally a contest between two men, Humphrey and Robert Kennedy, who had not been in the race a month earlier, and they were arguing over the ashes of the administration's foreign policy. Then, four days later, Dr. Martin Luther King was shot to death in Memphis. Within three hours, a riot broke out in Washington. In the following week, violence spread to more than a hundred cities.

If Johnson's March 31 speech seemed to leave in ashes the Democrats' postwar foreign policy, the April 4 King assassination and subsequent nationwide rioting seemed to leave in ashes their approach to black civil rights and poverty—major pillars of the Democrats' post-World War II domestic policy.

Long before his assassination, King's basic commitment—nonviolent demonstrations on behalf of black civil rights—had begun to seem irrelevant to many other black leaders, particularly younger ones. Passage of the civil rights bills had shifted the focus of public opinion toward the issue of poverty in general and black poverty in particular. Urban rioting and the quasi-separatist Black Power movement had called into question the viability of King's belief in Gandhian non-violence and racial integration. His death seemed to ratify and complete those trends. It was seized on by many blacks— including, it seemed, those who immediately took to the streets— as an end not just to the strategy of non-violence, but almost equally to the alliance between blacks and white liberals that had dominated the Democratic party's domestic agenda in the 1960s.

1968: HUMPHREY AND KENNEDY

If one man could be said to personify postwar Democratic liberalism, it was Hubert Humphrey. Although never president, he spanned the era more completely than any of the four Democrats who did become president in the liberal-dominated New Deal era (1932–68). Roosevelt died in office in 1945 and Truman left office with low popularity in 1953. Truman's handpicked successor as Democratic nominee, Adlai Stevenson, was almost exclusively a figure of the 1950s, and the two later liberal presidents, Kennedy and Johnson, were not widely regarded as liberal leaders until the 1960s.

Humphrey, by contrast, was intimately involved in all the postwar liberal causes, spanning more than thirty years. In the mid–1940s, his efforts to purge the Minnesota Democratic-Farmer-Labor party of communists made him a leading figure among liberal anti-communists. In 1948, as mayor of Minneapolis, his electrifying speech at the Democratic National Convention was a turning point in committing his party to the cause of black civil rights. He was a key drafter of much postwar Democratic social legislation as well as originator of the idea of the Peace Corps. A strong backer of containment, he was a vociferous down-the-line supporter of Johnson's Vietnam policy in his years as vice president.

If one word could sum up Humphrey's style, it was optimism. Going by the definitions of this book, Humphrey was strongly populist *and* strongly elitist, because, like much of New Deal liberalism itself, he was optimistic about average Americans and optimistic about the ability of elites to ameliorate the lives of average Americans. It would take much analysis to determine where these two values ran up against each other and how many times each tendency prevailed, but few would doubt that Humphrey was completely committed to *political* populism, whose hallmark is faith in the judgment of the electorate and the efficiency of the democratic system itself.

Humphrey's announcement for president on April 27 was of a piece with his personality and his entire political career. In his mind, the can-do attitude of postwar liberalism was intact, and his own exuberant optimism expressed itself as he proclaimed "the politics of joy."

The speech received perhaps the worst reviews of any announcement speech by a major presidential candidate in American history. It generated derision and rage throughout the elite opinion stream, but most particularly the liberal portion of it. The consensus among liberal elites was that in the era of Vietnam and ghetto rioting, there was little if anything to be joyful about.

The attack on the Humphrey announcement marked an attitudinal sea change for New Deal liberalism. In a way that proved deeper than a temporary (and understandable) reaction to the social chaos of 1968, the jaunty optimism of FDR and his successors was giving way to a darker, more pessimistic view among liberal elites. Post-1968 liberalism increasingly emphasized the limits of political action, and—particularly as it became evident that Republicans had established dominance in presidential elections—a more skeptical view of the American electorate as well. This dovetailed with growing elitism in the elite opinion stream in general and among liberal elites in particular: attacks on such phenomena as thirty-second television commercials and the growing power of presidential primaries implied increasing pessimism about voters' ability to make intelligent choices about their future.

But the pessimism inherent in the liberal attack on Humphrey also pertained to the other side of his optimism: his optimism about the ability of elites to provide answers for the people—that is,

Humphrey's New Deal-style liberal elitism. Coming in the same month as black rioting in more than a hundred cities, to many liberals an implicit rejection of their well-intended social engineering, Humphrey's confidence in old-fashioned, Washington-based programmatic liberalism seemed, if anything, even more outdated than his populist faith in the electorate.

Robert Kennedy's candidacy had a more contemporary look than Humphrey's. Kennedy was distinctly less sunny in substance and style than not only Humphrey but his own older brother. In part, no doubt, the turning to ashes of the liberal worldview on race and foreign policy dictated the change in tone. But Kennedy, more than any other liberal politician before or since, had become disillusioned with liberal elites and had a strong populist streak. He and his key younger advisors were influenced by the left populism of the 1960s, but—even in speeches that on the surface seemed radical—there was also a conservative element. According to speechwriter Adam Walinsky (as paraphrased by Theodore H. White in *The Making of the President—1968*):

The new radicals, said Walinsky one night in Indianapolis . . . had abandoned the old liberal ethos of centralization, the thought of Washington as the source of all national good. People had to be heard; people had to be met at the grassroots. Bobby, in Walinsky's view of his chief, had begun his separation from the old theories as early as 1965—with a first speech on education, advancing the thought that, just as schools test pupils, communities should be able to test their schools. A series of three speeches on the urban crisis had followed in 1966 elaborating another theme—that the welfare programs of the Federal government were no answer to the problems of the poor, but a positive destructive factor; the poverty program, for example, had hired thousands of middle-class people to tell poor people how not to be poor, a corps of "government-paid bitchers" competing to escalate their demands. All these thoughts, said Walinsky, were not new— they had come from the slow growth of observation on the part of Robert Kennedy once he had left the executive branch and observed the nature of executive power from the outside. But how does Kennedy's attack on central government differ then, I asked, from Barry

Goldwater's in 1964? Simple, answered Walinsky—Barry wanted to leave local institutions as they were, with local power as it was; we want to transfer more power to local institutions and change them at the same time. [32]

This passage is quoted not to argue that Goldwater and Robert Kennedy were political twins, or even that they both were thoroughgoing populists; neither one was, and Goldwater (in large part a product of Old Guard Taft conservatism) perhaps less so than the Robert Kennedy of 1968. But the fact that Kennedy and Goldwater sound most alike when their thought is most populist illustrates the depth of the liberals' 1968 crisis of confidence, and the extent to which liberalism's most creative minds were urgently trying to restructure their creed as the decade wore on.

Kennedy's 1968 campaign anticipated conservative populism on the social issue cluster as well. White describes in a footnote how Richard Nixon began emphasizing the law-and-order issue only after hearing Robert Kennedy's handling of it in the Oregon primary in late May: " . . . Kennedy had caught the strange, shapeless fear of violence in the American mind and had thus reoriented his campaign to stress his record as chief law-enforcement officer at the Department of Justice. . . . The feedback of the Kennedy campaign became apparent to Nixon only in his final telethon, in the contest on the Republican side of the Oregon primary. As the telephone calls piled up that evening for Nixon, he remarked, astonished, 'Do you know a lot of these people think Bobby is more of a law-and-order man than I am.' From then on, law-and-order became the prime theme of his campaign, and was to remain so to the end." [33]

Kennedy's brief campaign was an attempt not just to take the Vietnam issue from Eugene McCarthy but to counteract the mounting liberal demoralization caused by domestic violence and social breakdown. He was willing to acknowledge liberal failures on issues ranging from welfare to education to crime, and to structure new answers in a way that would keep intact the Democratic alliance between blacks and conservative-trending whites. His bridge between these two groups was not Vietnam dovishness but domestic populism, and the strategy showed considerable promise in a series of primaries culminating in California in early June.

Kennedy's assassination on the night of the California primary put a halt to that effort, not just for 1968 but (in large part) for the decades since. No subsequent liberal leader has made an effective effort to develop a form of left populism—and no liberal leader has come close to uniting blacks and Northern working-class whites, perhaps as a direct result. Subsequent polling in 1968 found many white Kennedy voters lining up for Richard Nixon and George Wallace, although, with great difficulty, Humphrey got some of them back by the November election. But no Democratic presidential nominee has ever done as well as Humphrey with these voters in the five elections since. In short, the effort to keep the Democrats' majority coalition together with a more populist appeal began and ended in the three months of Robert Kennedy's campaign.

Liberal Democrats had dominated American politics for thirty-six years, since Roosevelt's first election. Even in the eight-year Eisenhower interregnum, they largely set the issue agenda. Now, in little more than ten weeks between the New Hampshire and California primaries, the Democrats had seen (1) the collapse of their postwar foreign policy with the withdrawal of Johnson and his Vietnam reversal; (2) the collapse of the central assumptions of their postwar domestic policy with the black rioting following the assassination of Martin Luther King; to the point where (3) the optimism and high spirits shared by Hubert Humphrey and his New Deal-oriented counterparts seemed laughable. Now, on top of all that, the liberal standard-bearer who seemed to have the greatest chance of fashioning a new, attractive liberalism out of the ruins of the old had been struck down in the midst of his greatest victory.

The social upheaval of 1968 was widespread and cannot be easily summed up. But no group was more in flux than the elite opinion stream, particularly on the liberal side. As the sixties wore on, the alienation of campus and intellectual elites spread gradually into journalistic and political elites, culminating in Johnson's difficulty in recruiting elite support for his war policy. Sons and daughters of the most privileged of Americans manned the barricades of revolt, figuratively in the Democratic primaries and literally in the Columbia University riots of April, broken up by their social inferiors from the New York Police Department. It was the elite opinion stream that hooted down Hubert Humphrey's "politics of joy," marking the end of self-confidence on the part of the governing coalition. It was the elite opinion stream, embodied in newspaper editorials by Republicans as well as Democrats, that in March applauded the conclusion of the Kerner Commission that the cause of black rioting was the racism of most Americans. And it was the elite opinion stream that felt close to despair on the assassination of Robert Kennedy, the one emerging leader who seemed to have a chance of giving a new governing strategy to the thirty-six-year-old New Deal-era ascendancy. In June, as the nation approached a three-way choice among Richard Nixon, Hubert Humphrey, and George Wallace, it seemed that nothing more demoralizing could happen to liberals or to Democrats. In August, in Chicago, something did.

1968: CHICAGO

Before the Democratic National Convention in Chicago ended on August 29, 11,900 police, 7,500 U.S. army regulars, 7,500 Illinois National Guardsmen, and 1,000 FBI and Secret Service agents had been deployed to keep order in the streets. Television had beamed pictures of clashes between policemen and demonstrators into the homes of most American voters, and these pictures overwhelmed every speech and every event inside the convention hall.

The Republican convention, a month earlier in Miami, had delivered a television "bounce" in the polls to Richard Nixon, taking him from a virtual tie to a double-digit lead over Hubert Humphrey. But it was widely assumed to be a temporary effect. Other than war hero Dwight Eisenhower, a Republican nominee had not won a presidential election in forty years. Four years earlier, the Johnson-Humphrey ticket had taken 61 percent of the popular vote and forty-four of fifty states. Despite the obvious divisions in his party, Humphrey was widely expected to get his own "bounce" from Chicago and at least turn the race into the dead heat it had been before Nixon's post-Miami gains.

This did not happen. Nixon kept his double-digit margin until late October. At one point in the fall, right-wing Independent candidate George Wallace was within seven points of catching Humphrey in the Gallup poll (Nixon 43, Humphrey 28, Wallace 21). The Chicago convention had knocked the Democratic party almost unconscious; and Democrats have had few good experiences in presidential politics since.

The reaction of the electorate to the events in Chicago under-scored and perhaps deepened the split between the popular and elite opinion streams. Elite opinion tended strongly to sympathize with the mostly college-student demonstrators and to be furious with the police's tough, often violent suppressive tactics. This affected conservative as well as liberal elites. Hardly any *articulate* voice in August 1968 assigned more blame to the students than to the Chicago police and Mayor Richard Daley. The elite Walker Commission's eventual characterization of the episode as a "police riot" reflected well the reaction of the elite opinion stream.

Yet from the first polls, the overwhelming majority of the American people sided with the police. The police tactics, on television for all to see, had been raw, and the network and newspaper commentary on the tactics uniformly negative. Yet most people thought they were justified. It was as if everyone in America felt forced to make a choice between the police and the students. The choice people made in that moment proved predictive of their later political choices for years to come.

In particular, it affected the reaction of the two opinion streams to the Democratic party. In the short run, the Democrats lost ground with both opinion streams, but the reasons differed and so did the duration of the alienation.

Elite opinion was furious with the Chicago police and Mayor Daley, and to a lesser degree with Hubert Humphrey (who seemed at times to be a minor player in the week of his greatest triumph). Eugene McCarthy and some other leading liberal figures withheld their endorsement from Humphrey until late in the campaign. A few (such as columnist Walter Lippmann) even endorsed Nixon. But by November, few liberals had the heart to desert the Democratic ticket. In fact, the overall impact of the 1960s on elites wound up giving Humphrey better showings in elite-influenced districts than John F. Kennedy could boast against the same Republican nominee eight years earlier. As mentioned in the Introduction, Humphrey did far better in the nation's most elite congressional district, the Silk Stocking District on Manhattan's East Side, than Kennedy had done. Ivy League campuses that went overwhelmingly for Nixon in straw polls in 1960 gave him as little as 5–10 percent of the vote by 1968. Business elites were still Republican, but between November 1960 and November 1968, many other components of the elite opinion stream had shifted strongly toward the Democrats, regardless of the short-term impact of Chicago. By election day 1968, the long-term Democratic trend in elite opinion had firmly reasserted itself. However much such voters might be tempted to punish Humphrey, they were unlikely to find a favored vehicle in either the George Wallace campaign or in the increasingly conservative, Sun Belt-influenced Republican party.

The effect of Chicago on the popular opinion stream was less dramatic immediately, but ultimately far more profound. The vast majority of voters in "Middle America" (a term invented in the late 1960s by liberal columnist Joseph Kraft) sided with the police rather than the demonstrators. They certainly had doubts about the Vietnam War and the Johnson administration's policy on that and other issues, as demonstrated by the widespread popularity of Robert Kennedy prior to his assassination. But Hubert Humphrey's unwillingness to side with the demonstrators, which had angered many elite voters, certainly did not hurt him in Middle America.

Instead, popular opinion wondered why Humphrey didn't make a firm statement *against* the disorders that led to the battle with police. On an issue where everyone in the country seemed to have a strong opinion, Humphrey seemed to want to split the difference. To many voters, he appeared to be an emblem of the governing

Democrats themselves: unable to take sides, and thus no more able to end the rioting in their own convention city than the earlier rioting in black communities and college campuses. For all their difference in reaction to the events in Chicago, the one thing popular and elite opinion seemed to agree on was that Hubert Humphrey was not the man to bridge the cultural gap. This aspect of Chicago probably hurt Humphrey's candidacy more than anything else.

In the weeks after the convention, the performance of the Humphrey campaign appeared to accentuate all these popular doubts. Wherever Humphrey went, it seemed, he was greeted by deafening, sometimes violent anti-war demonstrators. At times he could not be heard by his audience at all. His valiant efforts to conduct a traditional liberal campaign in the midst of Democratic disunion won him a measure of sympathy with voters outside the anti-war orbit, and undoubtedly helped lay the groundwork for his fall comeback. But in the aftermath of Chicago the Democratic ticket suffered a hemorrhage of middle-class and working-class voters toward Nixon and Wallace. The national party that had received 61 percent four years earlier found itself through most of the general election at poll levels of 30 percent of the voters and under.

THE 1968 ELECTION

Given his fundamental decision to straddle the division in his party, Humphrey and his strategists had to find a way to bridge the values gap highlighted by the diametrically opposed reactions to the events in Chicago. Given that elites within the party were becoming more anti-war and more pro-student, the predominant advice Humphrey received was to move toward the anti-Vietnam position of the students.

But an outright break with the Johnson administration's war policy had grave risks of its own. There was, of course, the possibility that the President, still a powerful figure in the party and the country, would repudiate him. Furthermore, whatever doubts Middle America had about Vietnam, after Chicago they had even more about politicians who might seem ready to capitulate to the forces of the counterculture. (When George McGovern appeared to do this four years later, he met with little popular sympathy.) The strength of independent candidate George Wallace was spreading far beyond the segregationist South into blue-collar, unionized precincts all over the North. And unlike the 1964 primaries, when he had run against Johnson as the candidate of racial reaction, Wallace in 1968 was aiming almost all his rhetoric at long-haired demonstrators and "pointy-headed" professors and bureaucrats—the bedrock of the anti-Vietnam, pro-demonstrator wing of the national Democrats.

Wallace picked retired Air Force General Curtis LeMay, an advocate of massive bombing of North Vietnam, as his running mate for vice president, which cemented his appeal to hawks. But the major thrust of his rhetoric and appeal did not concern foreign policy but domestic values. He stood foursquare against the counterculture, and in favor of "law and order."

If Humphrey could reunite the Democratic party, he could win, as every Democratic nominee of the previous thirty-six years (except Adlai Stevenson) had done. But he was caught between Democrats who would have preferred Eugene McCarthy as the nominee and Democrats attracted to George Wallace or Richard Nixon; between Democrats who thought the United States was a corrupt society and a force for evil in the world, and Democrats who thought the United States was a good country whose basic values were under assault at home and abroad. To these latter Democrats, the Tet offensive, race riots, university takeovers by students, and the street battles at the Chicago convention were all of a piece, and they added up to one thing: the nation they loved was under assault and perhaps even in danger of chaos and collapse.

In the eye of the storm were the vice president and his running mate, Senator Edmund Muskie of Maine. They did their best to straddle the deep split in the party. In a celebrated incident that helped make him his party's front-runner for 1972, Muskie interrupted a speech to invite an anti-war heckler into a dialogue. On September 30 in Salt Lake City, Humphrey delivered a major speech on Vietnam saying he would take "risks for peace" by trying a temporary halt in the bombing of North Vietnam. This put some space between himself and Johnson without triggering an open break and appeared to give the campaign some momentum, according to mid-October polling. Rather than take a firm position on "law and order" that might go in the direction of either George Wallace or his opposite, Eugene McCarthy, Humphrey revived themes of earlier years that depicted Republicans as the party of economic privilege.

Given the condition of the party after Chicago, the Democratic campaign of 1968 was reasonably effective. Shortly before election day, President Johnson gave the ticket a boost by announcing a bombing halt similar to the one his vice president had suggested a month earlier. The AFL-CIO, perhaps at its historical peak in terms of political technique, reinforced Democratic campaign themes with unprecedented mail, telephoning, and workplace advocacy. The union movement was especially effective in countering George Wallace's appeals to working-class voters in the North. Richard Nixon, for his part, followed a strategy of sitting on his lead—avoiding debate with Humphrey and refusing to spell out a program, either domestic or foreign. Near the end, Humphrey came on with a rush, reducing a huge Nixon lead to virtually nothing in the closing weeks of the campaign.

Nixon's general election campaign was far from brilliant, nor was he "destined" to win. He ultimately won, not by default, but in a year when the Democratic party was showing more than a few signs of wishing to defeat itself. Late to the issue of "law and order," he wound up using it almost to the exclusion of everything else because he sensed the popular opinion stream's interest in it. Although the Democratic ticket made a determined effort to reknit the New Deal coalition, Nixon edged Humphrey in large part by becoming a respectable alternative to Wallace's raw social populism. He could have failed to win the needed majority of the Electoral College by losing closely contested California, but he did win 32 states to

Humphrey's 13 and Wallace's 5, even though his two opponents proved more impressive campaigners than he.

Nixon could have done better by taking risks—or possibly he could have lost by taking risks. He took no risks (not surprising for a candidate finding himself with a huge and unexpected lead the moment he was nominated), but instead went out of his way to depict himself as a candidate of stability, almost of the status quo.

But the status quo outlined by Nixon was in fact pro-change, not as a departure from the recent past but as a return *to* the recent past—the stable, cohesive past that preceded the fissures that had suddenly appeared in the American society of the 1960s. In competition with George Wallace, Nixon won just enough of the voters disturbed by the possibility of anarchy symbolized by Chicago to break the Democratic stranglehold on the presidency.

At the time of Nixon's victory, in November 1968 at the end of a year of shocks, it seemed probable that those circumstances would prove temporary. But for reasons that only gradually became clear, the partisan upheaval of 1968—rooted in simultaneous and cross-cutting realignments in the elite and popular opinion streams—would prove far from temporary.

CHAPTER 11

SPLIT-LEVEL REALIGNMENT, 1968–88

POST–1968 PARTY REFORM

Leading Democrats after 1968 made a great effort to avoid the kind of party split that culminated in Chicago. For aspirants to the presidency, that usually meant evading an overt break with the kind of activists who prevented Humphrey from being heard in his early speeches after Chicago. And this meant a move to the left in foreign policy and in domestic social policy. Most Democratic presidential candidates after 1968 defined "uniting the party" as preventing the alienation of the Left, which at this point in history happened to be highly activist and increasingly elitist. They less frequently defined it as winning back the middle-class and working-class voters whose defection had reduced the Democratic ticket from 61.0 to 42.7 percent of the popular vote and from forty-four to thirteen states between 1964 and 1968.

Even in 1968, the Democratic elites in charge of that year's convention—totally committed in most ways to the old-line Johnson-Humphrey hegemony—created what became known as the McGovern-Fraser Commission. Its mandate: to reform the presidential nominating rules of the Democratic party to make them more representative of the Democratic rank and file.

The McGovern-Fraser Commission defined this mandate as making sure that certain constituents of interest-group liberalism could not possibly be under-represented in any one state's delegation to the national convention. Such groups as women, blacks, Hispanics, and American Indians were mandated to appear in Democratic delegations in proportion to each group's share of the state's Democratic strength as a whole.

The massive move toward primaries between the 1968 and 1972 presidential cycles, it is frequently assumed, was mandated directly by the McGovern-Fraser Commission. In a sense this is true, but the commission itself did not mandate the primaries. Rather, a number of state parties reacted to the rigid quotas and guidelines of the commission by transforming themselves from convention to primary states. This was easy to do, because in most states Democrats controlled both houses of the state legislature. Whatever resistance state-level Republicans might have had to the pro-primary trend was overcome by state-level Democrats' need to conform with the McGovern-Fraser guidelines on proportional representation of certain groups within the population.

In fact, the movement of state-level Democratic establishments toward direct presidential primaries was not so much an acquiescence in the directives of the McGovern Commission as a defiance of them. In a sense, it was the last gasp of the old-fashioned party elites who had been the foot soldiers of Democratic national dominance between 1932 and 1968. Rather than agree to McGovern-style quotas, the old-line state Democratic establishments threw the presidential nominating process open to the voters—as the best option they could come up with to *defeat* the reformers.

The result of the McGovern Commission reforms, therefore, was twofold. First, it made state parties that were pro-reform more likely to conform to the demands of interest-group liberalism by picking delegations both "balanced" and (given the makeup of Democratic elites) more left of center.

Second, and more important, it populized the presidential nomination process as a whole by making primaries dominant. Beginning in 1972, a majority of delegates in each political party was determined by primaries. This represented an important breakthrough for the popular opinion stream. For the first time rank-and-file voters could overcome, rather than merely influence, the party's elites.

By way of contrast, in 1912—the first year presidential primaries were a factor—Theodore Roosevelt won nine primaries and 51.5 percent of the Republican vote, as against one primary and 33.9 percent for President William Howard Taft. But the unpopular Taft, supported by party elites, crushed Roosevelt for the nomination. In 1932, President Herbert Hoover was beaten decisively in seven primaries by Senator Joseph France of Maryland, yet was renominated virtually without opposition at the Republican convention that year. In 1952, Senator Estes Kefauver of Tennessee won twelve primaries but was defeated by Illinois Governor Adlai Stevenson (who had not entered a primary) on the second ballot. In 1956, Kefauver again dominated the primaries (though to a lesser degree), only to be defeated on the first ballot by Stevenson.*

In the pre–1972 politics of the Democratic party, McGovern's strong showing in the New Hampshire primary against front-runner Edmund Muskie might, in the cold eyes of history, have

* This is not to say that the introduction of presidential primaries was unimportant prior to 1972. In the four examples just mentioned, the nominees who lost the primaries suffered decisive defeats in November; in 1912, Taft's losses to Roosevelt provided legitimacy to Roosevelt's Bull Moose third-party candidacy, which in turn assured the election of Democrat Woodrow Wilson. New York Governor Thomas Dewey's victory over Harold Stassen in the 1948 Oregon primary was crucial to his nomination victory that year, and Dwight Eisenhower's primary victories over Robert Taft gave him momentum in 1952. That same year, Kefauver's upset victory in New Hampshire (however futile in terms of his own nomination) generated President Truman's withdrawal for renomination, much as McCarthy's strong showing against Johnson did sixteen years later. In 1960, John F. Kennedy used his primary strength against Humphrey and other challengers to turn key party elites toward his candidacy. Still it remains true that for pre–1972 candidates, primary victories had to be *combined* with elite support within the party. They could not by themselves nominate a candidate over the determined opposition of the elites.

amounted to very little—as little as the now-forgotten Joseph France's 1932 primary victories over Herbert Hoover. But given both the increased power of voters (in primary states) and of liberal elites (in states that had remained non-primary) in the wake of the McGovern Commission reforms, McGovern was able to stay alive until the April Wisconsin primary, which he won, setting off a chain reaction of elite party sentiment away from Muskie (and other traditional candidates, including the late-entering Hubert Humphrey) toward himself.

The ultimate victory of the McGovern Commission at the 1972 Miami convention was twofold: the populist revolution in the nominating system was vindicated by the upholding (on behalf of McGovern) of the winner-take-all rule of the California primary, rebuffing the Humphrey campaign's effort to obtain proportional representation of the results; and expulsion, on affirmative-action grounds (and also on behalf of McGovern), of the legally and democratically elected Daley delegates from Chicago, Illinois. Thus had power within the party come full circle in just four years. From the point of view of the party regulars who had nominated Stevenson, Kennedy, Johnson, and Humphrey, it was a demoralizing outcome: when they tried to be democratic in the old-fashioned way (in Illinois) they lost; when they tried to be democratic in the new-fashioned way (going for an exact representation of the overall vote shares in California) they were also rebuffed.

McGovern was, nonetheless, by any genuine yardstick the deserving nominee of the Democratic party in 1972. He won more primaries than any of his opponents, including less liberal party regulars Muskie, Humphrey, and Henry Jackson.

McGovern's overwhelming rejection by the popular opinion stream (he won 37.5 percent of the votes and just one of the fifty states) in the general election of 1972 did not impress Democrats as it might have, mostly because the Watergate scandal erupted on the heels of the election. The "dirty tricks" explanation of the 1972 outcome (together with recession and Republican policy retreat in 1973–75) enabled Democratic elites, in large part, to avoid analysis of the precipitous falloff in Democratic presidential voting (from 61.0 to 37.5 percent) between 1964 and 1972.

The Democrats' optimism was fortified when in the 1974 off-year election, in the wake of Nixon's resignation and in the midst of an inflationary recession, they gained a 2-to-1 advantage in Congress and a 3-to-1 lead in governorships. And when in 1976 they held onto these gains and elected a new president, Jimmy Carter, the two Nixon victories seemed to many Democrats an aberration.

Indeed, in the wake of the 1976 election it appeared quite possible that the post–1968 populization of the presidential nominating process would provide a net benefit to the Democrats. Carter, an "outsider" politician voicing vaguely populist themes, had used the open primary system to vanquish the candidates of the party left (Udall, Bayh, Harris, Shriver) and the candidate of the old-fashioned party regulars, Senator Henry Jackson of Washington. At the party's national convention in New York City, Carter had little trouble uniting the party's various factions.

Meanwhile, the Republicans' first full experience of an open primary-dominated system, the Ford-Reagan nomination battle, was closely divided and left far more visible wounds, particularly concerning foreign-policy issues where Reagan and Secretary of State Henry Kissinger seemed to be at polar opposites. At the Kansas City convention, Reagan asked not to be considered for the ticket, and his campaigning for President Ford in the fall seemed perfunctory and distant. It's unlikely Reagan could have emerged as such a strong candidate against a sitting president in the absence of the direct primary system instituted after 1968.

This, then, was the single most important outcome of the populist reform of the nominating process. For the first time in American history, party elites lost their veto over presidential candidacies. Because of the separation of the executive from the legislative branch, the U.S. system even before 1972 had already been far more open to outsider candidates than parliamentary systems in Europe and elsewhere. But starting in that year, the U.S. went even further on the path of political populism. For the first time, anyone—no matter how obscure or how unwelcomed by the party elites—could seriously contest the presidency and even prevail. The nomination of McGovern in 1972 and the strong showing of Reagan in 1976 underlined this new openness. The nomination and election of Jimmy Carter in 1976 proved that the new system could be conquered from beginning to end by someone completely unknown only a few months prior to his or her election. This made the American political system the most open in the world—meaning the most subject to influence by the popular opinion stream.

VALUES ISSUES AND REPUBLICAN DOMINANCE, 1968–88

While the emergence of Ronald Reagan onto the national scene may have been bad for Gerald Ford in 1976, it proved to be remarkably good news for the Republican party in the 1980s. In the three elections of that decade, the average Democratic ticket won 43 percent of the popular vote and carried six states for fifty-seven electoral votes (of a possible 538). Though they did not achieve realignment below the presidential level, Republicans went from a 2-to-1 deficit to rough parity in voter self-identification from early 1980 to late 1989. As a result of these elections, Republican strategists gained immense self-confidence in their ability to dominate the presidency, while leading Democrats gradually accepted the idea that their defeats of 1968 and 1972 represented not an anomaly but the beginning of a cyclical decline.

The pivotal event in this two-decade-old Republican hegemony was the nomination and election of Ronald Reagan in 1980. This election regained the presidency and was accompanied by the only significant Republican coattail effect since 1952, giving Republicans a net gain of 33 House seats and 12 Senate seats. Effective control of the House, coupled with a Republican majority in the Senate, gave Reagan the ability to enact major policy shifts in such areas as taxes and defense spending.

More than any of the four other Republican presidential wins since 1968, Reagan's 1980 victory involved major components of all three of the basic issue clusters: economics, foreign policy, and values. Concerning economics, much of Chapter 8 analyzes Reagan's use of his tax cut proposal to answer the valence issue of stagflation. In foreign policy, Reagan clearly gained by the seeming weakness of the Carter administration in the face of Soviet advances in the Third World and the Iranian hostage crisis. And in social policy, in 1980 a gulf opened up between Republicans and Democrats that was substantively greater than ever before.

In 1968 and 1972, Nixon's use of values issues was important, but not very specific. It didn't have to be, given the state of the Democrats in those two elections. In 1968 the theme of law and order was enough to convey to voters that Nixon intended to try to quell social unrest, without going as far as George Wallace might have gone.

In 1972, after a Republican recession, increased inflation, and a term of cultural strife centering on the issue of Vietnam, Nixon had reason to fear a united, moderately liberal Democratic campaign. Instead he got the McGovern candidacy, which he attacked with the negative, values-based epithet, "acid, amnesty, and abortion." At the 1972 Democratic convention, the same radicals who had been on the streets of Chicago four years earlier seemed all but in charge of the convention hall, and Middle America showed little sign of having warmed to them or to their values.

The Ford-Carter election of 1976 was a detour from the pattern. The two candidates' positions on abortion, for example, were virtually indistinguishable. If anything, Carter's evangelical Protestantism gave him a conservative cultural patina that (added to the central Republican vulnerabilities of Watergate and stagflation) played a role in putting him over the top.

But by 1980, evangelical and other social conservatives who had voted for Carter were having second thoughts. Unlike Ford, Reagan supported a constitutional amendment banning abortion, a position Carter opposed. Carter's Internal Revenue Service, moreover, had clamped down on private religious schools, helping to trigger the politicization of evangelical preachers and the founding of such groups as the Religious Roundtable and Moral Majority. And social conservatives of all kinds were affected by the increasingly permissive Democratic stance on drugs—a trend exemplified by Carter's White House drug advisor, Dr. Peter Bourne, who advocated the legalization of marijuana, said cocaine was non-addictive, and was finally forced to resign his position after improperly prescribing narcotics to a patient. On election day, Reagan carried the votes of 61 percent of born-again white Protestants, whereas Ford had won less than 40 percent against Carter in comparable polls four years earlier. The swing among these values-oriented voters was thus many times greater than the three-point Republican gain among voters as a whole (Ford: 48 percent; Reagan: 51 percent).

In 1984, Reagan continued to gain from all three issue clusters. As previously outlined, even though stagflation had passed from the scene, Mondale's decision to advocate higher taxes kept the economic issue alive. There were also clear disagreements in foreign policy, though perhaps not with the intensity of 1980 when such matters as Afghanistan and Iran were fresh in voters' minds. And on social issues, the gap between Reagan and Mondale was far wider than the gap between Reagan and Carter four years earlier.

In fact, one of the major surprises of the campaign was the emergence of values issues as a central topic of debate. Mondale and his running mate, New York Congresswoman Geraldine Ferraro, emerged from the July convention in San Francisco in fairly good shape. Virtually every poll showed Mondale still trailing Reagan, but some had him within a few points of the lead. And though Mrs. Ferraro was having trouble with her disclosure of financial records, she maneuvered around it in a skillfully conducted press conference a few days after the convention.

It was precisely at this point that she became entangled in a protracted exchange on her pro-choice position on abortion with several Catholic bishops, including New York Archbishop John O'Connor. Later, after his own nomination in Dallas, Reagan gave a speech defending the role of religious values in politics. For a time

Mondale strongly counterattacked, accusing Reagan of advocating a kind of religious test.

For around two months between July and September, and totally against advance planning in both camps, religion and values became the front-page news of the campaign. The polls of this period showed significant national gains for Reagan: in the South, where Reagan already had a solid lead over Mondale, he gained more ground, while on the East and West Coasts, Mondale scored slight gains, though not enough to bring him even with Reagan in either region. But in the Midwest—the one area of the country where Reagan's economic policies had not yet had a positive effect, and the area where his hawkishness was least popular—Reagan went from a virtual tie to double-digit leads. The race in such states as Michigan and Illinois was never again close.

By tacit consent of both campaigns, values issues waned between September and November. But the big lead Reagan had established over the summer was never shaken, even when he did badly in the first of the two national debates. Values issues were not the only ones working in Reagan's behalf, but they showed at least as great an ability to move voters as did the other two issue clusters. An exit poll showed Reagan's share of white evangelical voters—approximately a fourth of the electorate—soaring from 61 percent in 1980 to an extraordinary 81 percent in 1984.

1988: PURE VALUES ELECTION

Thus, while values issues were important in assembling Reagan's coalition in 1980 and 1984, they were still only one leg in a three-legged stool that also included economics and foreign policy. In the earlier Nixon victories, which began the Republican presidential advantage, values issues had been more dominant. Even Vietnam, a foreign-policy issue, had a values content that distinguished it from the earlier Cold War valence issue of how to contain communism while avoiding a world war. With the record Democratic-led expansion of 1961–69, followed by the Nixon recession of 1969–70, economic issues were of little if any net benefit to the Republicans in 1968 or 1972. Values issues were far more important.

Still, it can be argued that Nixon's victories were primarily a matter of Democratic disarray. They were caused not so much by a positive endorsement of the Republican response to the values issues as by a popular acknowledgment of Democratic self-impalement on the sword of those issues.

As for the 1988 election, perhaps its most interesting aspect is that none of the above caveats about the four Nixon and Reagan victories can be made. Unlike 1968 and 1972, the Democrats emerged from their convention with a united party. And unlike 1980 and 1984, the economic and foreign-policy issue clusters played relatively little role in the Republicans' solid forty-state victory.

Unlike Carter and Mondale, Democratic nominee Michael Dukakis avoided arguing for higher taxes while effectively describing his own commitment to economic growth (the "Massachusetts Miracle" was little challenged during the campaign itself). Furthermore, unlike McGovern and Mondale, the liberal Dukakis picked a conservative, hawkish running mate, Texas Senator Lloyd Bentsen. Given four increasingly cordial Reagan-Gorbachev summits in four years, and the signing of the first nuclear arms reduction treaty in history in 1987, Republicans were (perhaps ironically) not in a strong position to argue that election of a dovish Democrat like Dukakis would encourage Soviet aggression. In fact, the Republican campaign did little to make national security an issue. Four years earlier Reagan had been a passionate advocate of the Strategic Defense Initiative and Mondale had attacked him on it in a televised debate, but in 1988 no such highly charged foreign-policy disagreement emerged.

The Reagan years had brought peace and prosperity to the United States, and this framed the election. Yet peace and prosperity were roughly as evident in June as in November; in June Bush trailed Dukakis by seventeen points and in November he won by eight. In June, in leaning against Bush, voters were showing their typical future-orientation, the same syndrome that had cost a globally triumphant Winston Churchill the election of 1945. However appreciative voters may have been of the Republicans' successes in economics and foreign policy in the 1980s, it did George Bush little apparent good—until it was combined with other things.

The things that turned the 1988 election toward the Republicans had almost exclusively to do with values issues. These included Dukakis's membership in the American Civil Liberties Union, his veto of a bill mandating the Pledge of Allegiance in his state's public schools, his opposition to the death penalty, and (most prominently) his support for weekend furloughs for convicted murderers. Beginning around June, the Bush campaign began pushing these issues relentlessly, and in fairly short order Dukakis's big lead started to erode.

The attitude of the press and other elements of the elite opinion stream to these issues was not friendly. Most editors and commentators, Republicans included, had little sympathy for Bush's positions, and regarded the issues themselves as of minor importance. Furthermore, given Bush's background as an establishment Republican from an elite family, they had a hard time believing Bush was serious in espousing them. His status as the "respectable" half of the Reagan tickets had done little to prepare elite opinion for his aggressive use of values issues as a battering ram against the big Dukakis lead.

When it became evident that the Bush campaign had no intention of dropping them, and that Dukakis (despite many efforts) could not effectively combat them, the disdain of the elites turned to fury—at Bush and his top aides and, increasingly, at Dukakis and *his* campaign aides for their apparent impotence. Other targets included the producers of the advertisements, the rise of negative campaigning, and (at least tacitly) the gullibility and superficiality of the electorate itself.

The fact remains that Dukakis avoided obvious errors and carried far fewer liabilities than previous Democratic nominees of the

1980s. He never advocated a federal tax increase, he embraced economic growth, and he avoided a head-on challenge to the Reagan record on foreign policy, even picking a supporter of the Nicaraguan contras as vice president. He wrote off no section of the country, competing effectively in the Far West, where he wound up doing the best of any Democratic nominee since 1964. He handled his unpredictable chief nomination opponent, Jesse Jackson, adroitly in the primaries and at the Democratic convention, and made no serious errors in the debates with his Democratic opponents or Bush. Unlike George McGovern and Walter Mondale, he won raves for his selection of a running mate and conducted a full-scale campaign in the South.

His hemorrhage during the campaign was due not to ineptness or tactical errors, but to the substance of his positions on values issues, which could not easily be explained away. For, in contrast to the elites, the popular opinion stream did not seem to regard these issues as trivial. Republican peace and prosperity had not prevented the electorate from giving Dukakis a big lead over Bush in the spring, and the lack of a memorable clash on foreign policy and economics did not prevent the same electorate from swinging back to Bush by the late summer. It is hard not to conclude that 1988 was a year in which values issues dominated the debate and turned the electorate.

This is underlined by the impact of a values issue emphasized more by the Dukakis campaign than by Bush's: abortion. In the debates and in much of his campaigning, Dukakis aggressively defended a woman's right to choose and pledged to nominate Supreme Court justices who would vote to uphold abortion rights. Bush defended his anti-abortion position when challenged, but generally avoided raising the issue. Although prominent in the two nationally televised Bush-Dukakis debates, abortion attracted nowhere near the coverage attained by prison furloughs or the Pledge of Allegiance. Yet on election day, a *Washington Post*-ABC exit poll found that the issue of abortion was "very important" to 33 percent of all voters, and that Bush prevailed 57–42 percent among these voters.

The values root of Bush's victory was also clear in regional patterns. Bush did better than expected in states that were economically liberal but socially conservative—such as Pennsylvania and Michigan—while Dukakis exceeded expectations in California and Washington, which liked Reaganomics but were more liberal than average on values issues like abortion.

All in all, the 1988 election was unlike any other in the 1968–88 period of Republican presidential dominance in that it turned so exclusively on values issues. But in a larger sense, it was a reaffirmation of the roots of the post-New Deal alignment, which originated in the values crisis of the 1960s and in that decade's sharp divergence of the two opinion streams. In 1988 no less than 1968, a Democratic presidential campaign found itself unable to overcome the values gulf between the nation's elites and popular opinion.

SPLIT-LEVEL REALIGNMENT

In 1956, Dwight Eisenhower was re-elected in a landslide but Democrats scored slight gains at other levels of government. By that year, it was evident that split-ticket voting had become a major factor in the American political landscape. It set up the possibility of a political alignment in which one party could dominate the presidency while the other party held sway in Congress.

From the victory of Richard Nixon in 1968, and continuing to the present, such a political alignment has been a reality. Republicans have won five of six presidential elections, four times by landslides, while Democrats have controlled the House—never by fewer than fifty votes—and have had a majority of senators in all but three elections and a majority of governorships in all but one. Democrats have also dominated state legislatures and local offices.

Earlier in the cycle, many if not most analysts argued that this would prove temporary. Democrats might well regain the lock on the presidency they had enjoyed in 1932–68. As for Republicans, their presidential success, if sustained, would inevitably penetrate to lower levels. A third school, which included many respected political scientists and journalists, believed that the loosening of party loyalty had ushered in a period when party dominance of any sort would be unsustainable.

The elections of the 1980s were a blow to all these views. Three massive Republican presidential victories were accompanied by continued Democratic domination of Congress, governorships, and lesser offices. In 1968, it had been something of a shock when Richard Nixon won the presidency yet his party fell far short of winning either house of Congress. In 1988, George Bush carried forty of fifty states, yet the GOP saw its minorities *reduced* at every other level of government. Although it was the first time this had ever happened to a newly elected president, hardly anyone was surprised, much less shocked.

After twenty years and six presidential elections, the only theory left standing was that the United States was in a split-level alignment: Republicans normally won the presidency, Democrats predominated at all lower levels. Although in the 1980s Republicans won 133 of a possible 150 state presidential races (an astonishing 89 percent success rate), and Republican self-identification in the electorate grew to near parity, no significant dent was made in Democratic dominance below the presidency.

Now that the split-level nature of the 1968 realignment has been widely accepted, a number of theses have been forwarded to explain it. Most of them seem to beg the question. Partisan redistricting helps preserve Democratic dominance—but it does nothing to explain Democratic victories for governor, senator, and county offices. In recent years, campaign technology has given the advantage to incumbents, who have usually been Democrats—but it does not explain why Democrats have done just about as well in contests for open seats. Voters don't trust politicians and prefer to divide power between the parties—but in 1978 when voters had a chance to elect large numbers of Republicans to Congress to balance a Democratic White House, Republicans won only 158 House seats and forty-one senators—a gain of only eleven and three, overall a below-average off-year pickup by the party out of power. The only time in the entire twenty-year cycle Republicans *have* scored big sub-presidential gains was in 1980, when voters were ejecting a Democrat from the White House. Such facts cast considerable doubt on the supposed "balance of power" attitude of the electorate.

A theory that seems to cover more of the facts is that Republicans are better at articulating the electorate's broad values, while Democrats remain the "party of government"—the hard-headed practical pols who excel at bringing home the bacon to a given constituency. One test of this thesis would be whether the same value-affirming vs. constituency service pattern appears in analogous elections lower down the scale. Do Republicans do better in gubernatorial races than state legislative races? Do they do better in U.S. Senate than House races, given that Senate races tend to be somewhat more concerned with issues than constituency service?

The answer is yes. But their higher success rate in gubernatorial and Senate races (compared to state legislative and House races) has been minor compared to the advantage they have in presidential races. Beginning in 1968, Republicans have enjoyed an 83 percent dominance in presidential contests taking the nation as a whole and an 80 percent dominance in number of states carried, yet not much higher than 40 percent in any other category of election. Clearly, the rise of split-ticket voting since World War II made such a gap possible. But it doesn't explain why American voters since 1968 have so consistently taken full advantage of the possibility.

The central explanation of split-level realignment is the gulf that opened up in the 1960s between the elite and popular opinion streams. A populist-leaning conservatism gained the upper hand in the popular opinion stream, while an elitist-leaning moderate liberalism gained an even greater advantage in the elite opinion stream. And viable candidates for office originate almost exclusively in the elite opinion stream. Thus, given the overall leaning of elites since the 1960s, most serious candidates have naturally tended to be more liberal and elitist in their views than the electorate as a whole. Given the thousands of elective positions to be filled, the scarcity of populist-leaning conservatives in the elite opinion stream is a factor in and of itself.

But this numerical advantage among serious candidates, important as it is, does not ensure liberal or elitist victory in any one race. A conservative pursuing populist or anti-elitist themes can defeat conventional candidates if he or she can communicate directly with the popular opinion stream, over the head of unsympathetic political and media elites.

When Reagan ran, virtually all the other presidential candidates were more acceptable than he to elite opinion. And at least some of them, including the men he defeated in the 1980 and 1984 general elections, were smoother, less error-prone candidates. But Reagan overcame these disadvantages by establishing an issue-based rapport with the popular opinion stream.

Indeed, in all five Republican presidential victories since 1968, the winner campaigned against the grain of elite opinion. The one Republican who did not, Gerald Ford in 1976, was defeated by a Democrat who sounded quasi-populist themes.

Similar outcomes can happen and have happened in races for lower office. What is striking about the last two decades is how rarely this has happened. The kind of populist-leaning campaigns that dominated presidential elections have been far less frequent and far less successful in races for lower office.

In a period such as the 1950s in which the elite and popular opinion streams have broadly similar views, election of candidates with views in broad accord with popular opinion is the norm. Moreover, major-party candidates for the Senate, House, and other offices did not sound very different from Dwight Eisenhower and Adlai Stevenson, the Republican and Democratic presidential candidates of that decade.

In periods where the two opinion streams diverge somewhat more, however, the outcome of elections leans more toward popular opinion than the elites would like. In the 1930s and 1940s, when elite opinion was considerably to the right of popular opinion on economic issues, popular opinion opted for the liberal presidential campaigns of Franklin Roosevelt and Harry Truman five straight times. In congressional races, Democrats commanded nearly unbroken majorities, but after 1936 Republicans regained sub-presidential dominance in a majority of Northern states, and Congress became a stronghold of elite opinion's more conservative views on economic issues.

Since the 1960s, by contrast, a solid majority of elite opinion has been to the left of a solid majority of popular opinion. The gulf has been important on economic and foreign policy, but most striking—in 1988 no less than 1968—on values issues. The double realignment of the 1960s—popular opinion toward the populist center-right, elite opinion toward the elitist center-left—is fundamentally still in place. This explains why Bush was able to overtake and defeat Dukakis on issues such as the ACLU, the Pledge of Allegiance, and prison furloughs that the articulate segment of public opinion saw as mischievous or irrelevant. The phenomenon of double realignment also explains why Congress since 1968 has not only remained heavily Democratic, but has become considerably more liberal then it was in the era of Democratic presidential dominance.

The presidency gains the attention of the entire electorate, and only one competent candidate articulating socially conservative and/or populist themes need appear in the field every four years for the electorate to work its will. In the two decades of split-level realignment, moreover, the increased dominance of presidential primaries and television has further popularized the presidential process.

Candidates for lesser office have far less ability to gain the electorate's attention. Instead of a series of primaries, there is only one, and television coverage is unusual in races for U.S. House and below, and far from automatic in races for senator and even governor. Since 1976, too, a candidate for a presidential nomination has had access to matching government funds while candidates for Congress and most state offices have to raise money from the private sector.

A major consequence is that candidates below the presidential level are greatly dependent on various elites—consultants, journalists, business, labor, and all the rest—to get their candidacies taken seriously in the first place. And given the leanings of present-day elites, candidates and potential candidates are constantly pressured to become homogenized: liberal candidates are being advised to sound more populist to attract popular opinion, and conservative candidates to sound less populist to attract the elites—political, media, and financial—whose support or at least acceptance is important in getting a candidacy off the ground.

As a result, many campaigns wind up meeting, rhetorically, somewhere in the middle. Liberal candidates are more numerous and more competent, conservative candidates are more in tune with popular opinion. In many races, liberals wind up retaining more of their edge in competence than do their conservative opponents on issues, given the process of homogenization of rhetoric and issue positions. Conservatives struggle to underline their closeness to popular opinion, but this can be psychologically difficult for a performer whose day-to-day elite "audience" (in the term of sociologist Tamotsu Shibutani) constantly reinforces the values of elite opinion.

Not only do more liberals win than might be expected, given the views of the popular opinion stream, many conservatives, once in office, feel the same pressures toward homogenization as during the campaign process. The emergence of a challenger depends heavily on elites, so a conservative congressman or governor or state legislator tends to modulate his or her rhetoric in the direction of acceptability to the elite opinion stream. In most cases, the motive is not to give up or betray one's ideology, but to avoid attracting unfavorable attention from powerful elites that can threaten incumbency.

The result, though, is to reinforce the phenomenon of split-level realignment. The kind of ideological polarization that has aided presidential candidates like Nixon, Reagan, and Bush does not often extend to congressional campaigns or debate in Congress. And homogenized rhetoric and convergence of issue positions almost by definition favor the elite opinion stream with its deep supply of well-educated, polished candidates.

STABILITY OF SPLIT-LEVEL ALIGNMENT

There have been previous realignment periods in which the presidency took on a different ideological cast from lower levels of government. Andrew Jackson's 1824 plurality in the popular vote and Electoral College was overridden by Congress in favor of an aggressively elitist candidate, John Quincy Adams. Following his capture of the presidency in 1828, Jackson struggled through most of his two terms with a Congress that took elitist positions on the economic issues that dominated the day. Jackson's clash with Congress over the Bank Veto of 1832 shaped American politics for years to come. It was only after 1844, when Congress enacted the Jacksonian economic agenda of James Polk, that the 1828 realignment could be said to be complete.

Much of the New Deal era pitted a liberal presidency against a conservative Congress. Democrats swept the elections of 1932, 1934, and 1936 at every level. But a Republican comeback in the North began in 1938, and for the next few elections Republicans were able to dominate voting for the governorship, U.S. Senate, and U.S. House in most Northern states despite continued victories by Roosevelt and Harry Truman at the presidential level. The rise of split-ticket voting helped Northern Republicans do well at the subpresidential level even in presidential years.

The solidly Democratic South enabled Democrats to maintain overall congressional majorities, except in the elections of 1946 and 1952. But for many years, enough conservative Democrats were elected to give conservatives a working majority in Congress against both Roosevelt and Truman. In these cases, a nominally Democratic but conservative Congress usually thwarted a liberal presidency. As discussed in Chapter 9, the deadlock also reflected a significant split between the popular and elite opinion streams, particularly on economic issues.

In *Dynamics of the Party System*, James Sundquist has described how the New Deal revolution gradually triumphed at the sub-presidential level between 1948 and 1964. A new type of Democratic candidate—called by Sundquist "programmatic liberal Democrats"—began to win elections in the North in states that had previously been Republican at the sub-presidential level. In the Congress elected in 1964, New Deal-style liberalism was able decisively to outvote the conservative coalition and enact its unfinished agenda—not simply because Congress was more heavily Democratic but also because of the more ideological type of Democrat now representing the North. Sundquist called this process "second-stage realignment."[34]

So in the Jackson and Roosevelt alignments—the two previous eras in which Congress was ideologically different from the presidency for extended periods—the Congress became more closely aligned with the presidency. In both cases, as might be expected, this evolution roughly coincided with convergence of the popular and elite opinion streams. Beaten repeatedly in presidential politics, elite opinion began to accept Jacksonian economics in the first instance and New Deal-style big government in the second. In the New Deal era (1932–68), the only previous alignment affected by the phenomenon of widespread split-ticket voting, a mild movement to the left in the elite opinion stream helped bring significant election gains in a majority of the country to the kind of liberal Democrats who had earlier achieved mastery of the presidency.

Nothing resembling this has happened in the post-New Deal alignment that began with the election of 1968. There has been no erosion either of populist conservative dominance of presidential elections or of elitist liberal domination of Congress and other levels of public office. If previous patterns had been followed, elite opinion should have evolved toward a greater acceptance of conservative-leaning populism; or, alternatively, presidential politics might have moved back toward dominance by elite opinion, whether in the form of liberal Democrats or establishment Republicans of the Eisenhower-Ford stamp.

In fact, neither has happened. While the conservative populist presidency won some key victories on the floor of Congress, particularly in the Reagan years, Congress is today about as Democratic and somewhat more liberal than in the 1960s. And while a Republican of establishment background, George Bush, was nominated for president in 1988, he employed conservative values issues to win the general election. Upon election, he found himself confronted by a strongly Democratic Congress with its own agenda—just as Richard Nixon had twenty years earlier.

For more than two decades, elite opinion has remained elitist and popular opinion has remained populist. The existence of split-ticket voting all through the period has given the split between the two opinion streams a more explicitly partisan shape than during the Jackson and Roosevelt periods. But the fact remains that the polarization of the two opinion streams—and the extraordinary persistence of this polarization—is what has made the rest of the political landscape possible. The fundamental difference between the 1968 alignment and the previous alignments is that in the previous eras the two opinion streams converged, and in this era they haven't. Why?

NIXON: ABORTIVE REALIGNMENT

One clue may lie in the simple fact that the first presidency of the 1968 alignment, that of Richard Nixon, ended in failure. All previous partisan realignments—marked by the election of Thomas Jefferson in 1800, Jackson in 1828, Lincoln in 1860, William McKinley in 1896, and FDR in 1932—led off with effective presidencies. The first two, Jefferson and Jackson, left office after two successful terms having dictated their successors; the last three died in office at the height of their popularity and political mastery.

Nixon had one thing in common with the five earlier realignment presidents: he won re-election by a landslide. But, in his case, eighteen months into his second term he was forced to resign under threat of impeachment in connection with the Watergate scandal. Unlike the five earlier presidents, his party lost the White House in the first election in which he was not on the ballot.

Nixon's presidency was abortive in a second sense as well. It failed largely to fulfill his central mandate from 1968: to govern against the grain of America's increasingly liberal elites. On issue after issue, Nixon adopted the framework of 1960s liberalism: on economic issues, he imposed wage-and-price controls and embraced Keynesian deficit spending; on foreign policy, he accepted Soviet missile superiority in the arms-limitation talks and pursued détente with Maoist China; and on social policy he promoted a guaranteed annual income proposal he had ruled out in his campaign. Even on issues where he resisted the elites—such as his attempt to preserve the anti-communist government in South Vietnam while withdrawing American soldiers, and his attempt to remake the liberal Warren Court with conservative Supreme Court appointments—he found himself in bloody battles with Congress and to a considerable degree thwarted. Nixon left office with a stagflationary economy, a precarious peace settlement in Vietnam that left several hundred thousand North Vietnamese troops in position to mount a final attack on South Vietnam, and a Supreme Court that (in such decisions as the 1973 decision mandating abortion on demand in all fifty states) seemed as capable as ever of legislating from the bench.

In each of these respects, Nixon's failure was liberalism's success. First, Nixon adopted many of the liberal policies he had campaigned against. Second, he was at least partially thwarted in the areas where he tried to resist liberal elites. Third, his presidency ended in disgrace to the applause of most of those same elites. In earlier realignments in which presidents had to govern amid the strong opposition of contemporary elites—Jackson and FDR—the elites had been demoralized by successful presidencies. At the outset of the most recent realignment, the adversarial elites of Nixon's day found themselves energized by an unsuccessful presidency. Given the respect for power of most elites at most times, the same factor that influenced the earlier elites into alignment with the popular opinion stream served to maintain the gulf in post–1968 public opinion.

REAGAN AND THE ELITES

The memory of Nixon's failure kept liberal morale higher than it otherwise would have been during its subsequent two ordeals: the failure of the Carter presidency, followed by the success of the Reagan presidency against the predictions of most elites. All through the Reagan years, liberals succeeded in maintaining great influence in Congress and the near-total allegiance of such institutions as the media and education. Reagan may have been unusually successful in setting the agenda and achieving his major goals, but the elite opinion stream never showed much sign of adjusting or modifying its view of Reagan or his policies. Even when Reagan's economic and foreign policies began showing results that impressed public opinion as a whole, liberals remained unimpressed and ready to fight on multiple fronts.

Yet if the liberals' thwarting of Nixon kept alive their hopes that Reagan would meet the same fate, one would nevertheless have expected that their failure to thwart Reagan in the battle for public opinion would have had at least *some* countervailing effect—that is, Reagan's successes should have caused some erosion in liberal self-confidence and in liberal mastery of the elite opinion stream. There is little evidence that it did.

It is not that Democrats in Congress made no adjustments. Liberals who had violently attacked Reagan's 23 percent cut in average tax rates spread out over four calendar years (1981–84) found themselves supporting a far deeper cut in tax rates (including a 44 percent cut in the *top* tax rate) phased in over just two years (1987–88). But liberals could argue that in the Tax Reform Act of 1986, the ending of various deductions counter-balanced the rate reductions, thus making the tax code more progressive. So even though the core policy result of the two landmark tax bills was similar—massive rate reduction—liberals were able to participate in the second phase of 1980s tax cutting without giving up their *ideological* opposition to this major theme of the Reagan presidency.

Similarly, liberal Democrats such as Edward Kennedy who had attacked Reagan's domestic spending restraint in his first term found themselves supporting the conservative Gramm-Rudman-Hollings deficit reduction plan in 1985, arguing that in the second case the defense budget would be affected about as much as domestic spending. But they remained as critical as ever of Reagan's restrictive domestic budget policies.

In the defense and foreign policy area, Reagan in 1982 was widely criticized by liberal elites as inflexible for proposing a "zero option" on the issue of U.S. and Soviet middle-range missiles in Europe. They became warm supporters of "zero option" when Soviet leader Mikhail Gorbachev agreed to the same plan in the Intermediate Nuclear Forces (INF) Treaty of 1987. But few of them altered their view that Reagan's foreign policy was dangerously hawkish.

In terms of overall outcome, few presidents have enjoyed Reagan's success in economic and foreign policy. The last six years of his presidency saw the longest peacetime expansion in American history and the creation of nearly twenty million new jobs with low inflation. Foreign policy saw U.S.-Soviet relations move from confrontation to the winding down of the Cold War, including increasingly friendly Reagan-Gorbachev summits in each year of Reagan's second term.

Yet most elites, and not just liberal elites, rated Reagan about as low on economic and foreign-policy management at the end of his term as they had at the beginning. Even when acknowledging the positive trends, elites tended to credit factors other than Reagan's performance. By contrast, public opinion as a whole gave Reagan the highest favorable rating ever received by a president leaving office.

Who was right or wrong on these issues—or how much credit Reagan deserved for favorable outcomes where these could not be disputed—is beside the point, at least from the standpoint of the gulf between the popular and elite opinion streams that has existed since the 1960s. The fact is, even in cases (such as reduced tax rates) where Reagan prevailed, the elite opinion stream did not change either its disapproval of Reagan or its ideological commitment to the idea which had met defeat. Earlier elites that had opposed Jacksonian economics or New Deal reforms had eventually realigned toward the views of the winning side. But present-day elites have been loyal to their belief system even when facets of it seemed to have become politically dangerous.

The anti-Reagan elites would probably not have been able to maintain their morale in the face of their setbacks in economic and foreign policy unless, in some deeper sense, they felt they were winning. It was on the third major issue cluster—values issues— that this remained the case throughout the 1980s.

THE VALUES BATTLEFIELD

By a number of measurements, Reagan made progress on the values front. He filled three Supreme Court vacancies with judicial conservatives and elevated the most conservative previous appointee, William Rehnquist, to the position of chief justice in 1986. By the end of his second term, Reagan had appointed approximately half of the federal judiciary. As a result, by the measurement of social populism discussed in Chapter 3—the ability of people to set their own standards—a number of issues came increasingly under popular control as the 1980s wore on.

But while the judiciary has been the main institution preventing restoration of popular control over community standards, it is by no means the only institution with influence over what those standards are. The continued dominance of liberal elitism in the elite opinion stream meant that journalistic, entertainment, artistic, educational, and other elites were as much a force against traditional values as ever. Indeed, as older and less liberal individuals have retired from these professions, elite conformity on a number of key values issues has increased. This has had a wide impact.

Polls and sociological studies confirm that on such moral/behavioral issues as divorce, abortion, homosexuality, and nonmarital sex, the permissive attitudes of elite opinion became more widespread during the 1980s among public opinion as a whole and—most disturbingly for social conservatives—among high school and college students when compared to their predecessors a decade earlier. Moves away from permissiveness on violent crime and illegal drug use showed that the values trend could shift in either direction, but provided scant consolation to advocates of traditional values in the context of the cultural battlefield as a whole.

This was particularly true for social conservatives because of the bleak outlook in the most future-oriented of all elite institutions: education. The faculties and curricula of elite universities—the earliest targets of the radical values challenge of the 1960s—had moved very far in a quarter century. Many of the same students who had led the New Left challenge to the earlier educational establishments had ascended to power in those establishments in the 1980s. These elites were far from intimidated by Reagan's popularity in the popular opinion stream, or even by the following he gained among undergraduates. As the 1980s came to a close, educational elites at all levels of university and public education were moving to transform curricula in the direction of liberal elitism, not just in terms of viewpoints but even of the subjects allowed to be studied. Reagan's second-term education secretary, William Bennett, was a persistent critic of these trends, and as a result became a complete outsider among educational elites.

Bennett was unusual among conservative elites in wanting to contest such issues at all. Even during the Reagan years, most Republican and conservative leaders tended to de-politicize values issues altogether (except in presidential election years when they could come in handy against candidates like Dukakis). They argued that the less divisive economic and foreign-policy issues were more fundamental to the Republican presidential dominance of the 1980s, and that as long as they maintained their advantage on these issues in public opinion they could afford to treat most if not all moral/behavioral issues as part of private life rather than as part of politics.

A number of liberal Democratic leaders agreed in wanting to

relegate values issues to a back burner, albeit for somewhat different reasons. Just as Republican elites regarded values issues as divisive within their coalition, these Democrats found mirror-image divisiveness among *their* voters. Evidence suggested that candidates like Mondale and Dukakis had been on the defensive in middle America and had done badly among such traditional Democratic groups as Southern whites and Northern blue-collar workers, particularly when values issues had the center stage. Many of these Democrats argued that their party's big troubles had started when their presidential candidates got on the wrong side of values issues in the 1960s and early 1970s, and advocated more attention to the kind of economic issues that had served candidates like Roosevelt, Truman, and Kennedy so well in the 1932–68 era of Democratic presidential dominance.

A major problem with such a Democratic strategy is that it goes against the grain of the post–1968 alignment and of the 1960s revolution in the elite opinion stream that triggered it. As described in Chapter 10, the failure of left populism to attract a following in popular opinion following the worldwide upheavals of 1968 meant that, from then on, the Left turned much of its attention to its critique of traditional values and became increasingly elitist in its attitude to the popular opinion stream. In the United States this turn might have been averted had Robert Kennedy lived, but his death in June 1968 left no populist or quasi-populist heirs among liberal leaders in this country. Four years later, the elevation of George McGovern confirmed the elitist, countercultural thrust of the post-Robert Kennedy American left.

As a result, it is fair to say that the liberal majority of the elite opinion stream today is far more ideologically engaged on values issues than on any other. The kind of passion that went into the battle against the Robert Bork and Clarence Thomas nominations or for abortion rights is seldom matched by liberal passion on foreign policy or economics. Liberal elites, furthermore, have been able to rally significant elements of the popular opinion stream even on values issues that seem inherently unpopular. These include opposition to a constitutional amendment banning flag burning and defense of government-subsidized art regarded as obscene or sacrilegious.

The elite opinion stream is bigger in the United States than in any previous society. As discussed in earlier chapters, this is in large part because the United States is the wealthiest and most complex society in history. When it becomes self-confident on an issue cluster—in this case because of its degree of commitment and its significant successes in popular opinion—elite opinion tends to intimidate even those elites (business and religious elites, for example) that normally have reservations about liberal positions. This leaves political elites who wish to take the traditional side of values issues with little or no reinforcement. It is no small thing that taking a traditional position on such matters as homosexuality or abortion confers low status in elite circles.

Perhaps ironically, the degree of Reagan's success in the economic and foreign-policy issue clusters is what makes continuation of the values war unavoidable. This is in part because progress on valence issues like the Cold War and double-digit inflation makes values issues by far the most contentious; and in part because the current split-level alignment has a values root dating from the 1960s, whose core values conflicts have remained unresolved.

But it is also because of the power of the classical view of politics itself, as outlined in Chapter 3: the setting of a society's standards is, in the final analysis, what politics is about. Because of events around the world, it seems increasingly possible that the standard-setting view of politics—so long in eclipse—is on the verge of becoming more compelling than ever before.

CHAPTER 12

POLITICS IN THE AGE OF EQUALITY

THROUGHOUT HISTORY, politics has been the means of determining a community's way of life. Individuals of course make important decisions outside politics—including what most people at most times have regarded as the most important ones, on such subjects as worship, love, and family life. But for those (nearly everyone) who live in a political community, politics sets those standards that affect each member of the community and—at least potentially—it can enhance, discourage, or even prohibit social activities that are non-political in nature. In this sense few would disagree with Aristotle that politics is the master science of the good.

For most of history, elites controlled politics and set community standards. A people's way of life could change because a king changed religions or lost a war. Islam converted much of Eurasia by the sword and came within an eyelash of losing it to the pagan Mongols in the thirteenth century. In just a few decades Islam recovered and extended its sweep because its advocates outperformed Christian missionaries in the command centers of a handful of Mongol chieftains thousands of miles apart.

The central event of the twentieth century has been the spread of the idea of innate equality—equality that must be recognized *in the present*—to most of the world. Once equality in this sense of irreducible human dignity has been widely accepted in a community, it is only a matter of time before it becomes the cornerstone of politics. Regardless of what might be the case in religious, professional, or family life, where different people may have different standing, innate equality will inevitably be recognized in politics, the area of life that applies to the community as a whole. The adoption of democracy in country after country is and will be the result.

This means that more and more of the world's people will participate directly in choosing their own community's standards. In theory, they could delegate this task to political, judicial, religious, or other elites and wind up having almost as limited a role as in the period before the victory of political equality. But because of its greater vulnerability to public evils, the popular opinion stream is more interested in issues than in the political "horse race" that fascinates elites. This ultimately means that there will be popular debate and decision-making about the community's goals and values.

In regimes of political equality, elites are important in setting standards. They are important because they have political and other expertise and because they can set examples on values and life-styles for popular opinion to observe and follow. But elites that want to set standards must now operate mainly by persuasion. Electorates will often allow elites to participate in setting and enforcing standards, but they will do so consciously and with greater knowledge of what is happening. There will be much less *political* deference to the blood, knowledge, religious, and other elites that held sway in the age before equality.

Popular standard-setting becomes more prominent with the rise of pluralism. In nations where the population is culturally and racially homogeneous, as in Confucian China for much of its history, the people's way of life and belief system tend to be secure and taken for granted, and thus can remain outside active politics. With pluralism—which frequently accompanies political equality—differing value systems are well represented within a single electorate. Politics must serve as the arbiter when widely different concepts of community standards clash.

As Robert Kelley recounts in *The Cultural Pattern in American Politics*, the struggle over community standards among different religious, cultural, and ethnic groups has been a pivotal factor of American political identity from the beginning—including the early nineteenth century when virtually the entire U.S. electorate consisted of white Protestants. Voters' positions on such values issues as religious establishment, closing of businesses on Sunday, public drinking, and slavery showed high correlation with their denomination and ethnic group. Issues of this type were, moreover, highly predictive of whether a given voter was a Jeffersonian Republican or a Federalist. In Massachusetts, a Calvinist of English ancestry was likely to be a Federalist who favored a state church, temperance, blue laws, and abolition of slavery. In New York, a German Lutheran was likely to be a Jeffersonian with the opposite view on all these subjects.

In the past fifty years, ethnic and religious background as a predictor of values allegiance has eroded in the United States. Intermarriage has increased sharply. Fifty years ago, surveys have shown, an Italian-American was overwhelmingly likely to marry another Italian-American; today, an Italian-American is overwhelmingly unlikely to do so. Twenty-five years ago, Catholics were more likely to oppose legalized abortion than were Protestants. Today, with the national division at least as intense, Catholics are not much likelier than Protestants to do so. Each generation—and each individual within his or her generation—appears to feel much more free to choose his or her view of community standards and his or her way of life.

Pluralism is starting to arrive elsewhere. In the immediate post-World War II period, a country like France was composed almost wholly of people of French descent. With the end of European imperialism and the rise of the Common Market, this is less and less the case. The trend toward European pluralism will undoubtedly accelerate with full economic integration after 1992, when most remaining barriers to emigration and multinational economic activity disappear.

In the world of equality and global communications, decisions about both individual and community standards become less and less predictable by geography, ethnicity, and social class. The world is no longer shocked to see millions of Latin Americans becoming Protestants, or an entire generation of elites in Eastern Europe discarding Marxism in the years prior to the democratic revolutions of 1989.

With the spread of democracy and pluralism in the world, standard-setting will likely be more peaceful than it was in the age of monarchy and empire. Does this imply that values issues will prove less contentious or less central?

In fact, it stands to reason that with the Cold War over and a global consensus taking hold in favor of mass democracy and more or less free economies, values issues are the biggest remaining bone of contention in politics. The decline of ethnocentric belief systems and the rise of pluralism implies further that standard-setting must take place anew in each generation—or, to look at it another way, will be fought out intensely in politics until such time as democratic communities around the world arrive at standards that seem compelling enough to fix. As discussed at the end of Chapter 3, fixing standards in politics usually means enacting them in written constitutions that are difficult to amend.

In Eastern Europe, values issues began to erupt as soon as it became clear that the communist systems had been definitively defeated—a remarkable development considering the depth of those countries' economic problems. Such issues as the role of religion in Hungary's schools and abortion in Poland immediately began to divide previously united anti-communist coalitions. Conflicting abortion laws, not economic issues, proved to be the final sticking point in the merger of East and West Germany in 1990.

In the United States, most of the elite opinion stream is strongly opposed to this kind of values combat, as it made clear by its disdain for the issue selection of the Bush campaign in 1988. The first line of defense against the politicizing of such issues—a federal judiciary that consistently threw out efforts of state and local communities to set their own standards on such values issues as abortion and pornography—is eroding due to the appointments of Presidents Reagan and Bush. But the second line of defense of liberal elites against an upsurge of values politics is at least equally impressive, in that it is based on a firmly believed, understandable idea rather than the raw power of judicial elites. This line of defense is their widespread propagation of the idea that all moral values are relative, and that accordingly very few if any should be adopted by the community acting together.

Relativism has roots much earlier than the twentieth century, but this is the century in which it has flourished, particularly among elites but also within a significant segment of the popular opinion stream. Perhaps an important reason lies in the history of science.

It has often been remarked that Newtonian physics, with its mechanistic, cause-and-effect universe, influenced the rise of Deism and its detached God-as-watchmaker, as well as related political and economic theories. Chapter 4 mentions how the charismatic success of Darwinian biology—in particular the concept of natural selection—helped popularize the earlier Hegelian idea of political and economic progress through conflict.

In this century, the analogous development is Einstein's Theory of Relativity. It was during the dissemination of Einstein's work that prestige historians turned away from the earlier "Whig interpretation"—history as the progressive advance of Western-style political liberty—toward a view of world history as the rise and fall of vastly different civilizations. This change in the philosophy of history was accompanied by the idea of cultural relativism— that no society can or should be taken as necessarily superior to any other.

In addition, cultural relativism was gaining ground at a time when Western civilization, previously assumed to be the highest organism of social evolution, seemed to be tearing itself apart in world war and depression. World War I, in particular, shattered the self-confidence of Western elites, putting an abrupt end to the idea of history as a march of progress toward Western ideals.

But the world wars also aided relativism in a different way. World War I dealt the death blow to ruling monarchy in Russia, Germany, Austria-Hungary, and the Ottoman Empire. This (together with the 1911 overthrow of the two thousand-year-old Chinese imperial system) effectively ended ruling monarchy as a vibrant institution and put the idea of political equality on the world's agenda in a way it had never been before. The fascist movement was a non-monarchical attempt to push it back off the agenda, but by 1945 this effort had utterly failed.

A strong case can be made that the idea of universal human equality most logically belongs in politics, the only area of social life in which all people have equal standing as members of a community. But, as Tocqueville predicted in the early decades of American and French mass democracy, equality is too powerful an idea to be contained in politics alone.

Much of this century's battle has been about the extent to which equality should apply to the field of economics. The discrediting of radical socialism around the world, though the major event of this century's second half, does not appear to have ended the ideal of equality of economic result. In American political debate (and in democracies as far away as India), the drive for employment quotas is very much alive. So are arguments for using the tax code and government spending to achieve greater equality of result.

Equality of result—which, as discussed in Chapter 1, by definition implies managing toward equality by an elite, and therefore elitism—also has support in the field of political procedure. In European democracy, this has often taken the form of proportional representation, the attempt to match the exact voting strength of political parties with representation in parliaments. Not coincidentally, this practice usually has the effect of fostering brokered rule by legislative elites. In the United States, equality of political result often takes the form of reapportionment lawsuits to mandate that black, Hispanic, and other minorities attain election outcomes consistent with their share of the population.

In the realm of moral values, a belief in equality of result demands the victory of relativism in society. That is, equality of result means that no one's moral belief system must in the end be elevated above anyone else's. This in turn implies that it is illicit for a community to set moral standards beyond the most rudimentary needed to prevent violence.

So the application of the elitist vision of equality—managing toward equality of result—can be seen as twofold. In economics, political procedure, and other areas outside the values issue cluster, the standard is equality of result. In the moral realm, the standard is relativism—or, to put it in moral terms, tolerance. These are the two distinctive standards favored by liberal elites today. It would be difficult to find in contemporary political debate an issue position regarded as distinctively liberal that does not trace back either to equality of result or to relativism, which at root are the same thing.

Environmentalism, for example, does not at first glance appear to have anything to do with the concept of equality. But, at least for many liberals, this issue has become deeply bound up with their commitment to relativism. Liberal environmentalism is committed to the idea that in the relationship between humanity and the other components of nature, humanity should not be given priority. This is why, in the 1960s and 1970s, the actual label of this issue cluster gradually changed to "environmentalism" from "conservation," a term which implies the Judaeo-Christian belief in the priority of human needs over those of the rest of nature. More recently, the rise of the animal-rights movement has had an even more explicitly relativist cast. Animal rights is in large part a subset of cultural relativism in which animal societies are given equal standing with human society.

The issue of increased urban homelessness, if it had arisen in the 1950s or earlier, would have been seen as a straightforward valence issue—that is, an agreed-on public evil where the debate would be mainly over what measures were needed to bring it to an end. It is in part that today. But since it arose in the 1980s, it became to a surprising degree a values issue, in which liberal elites have asserted that the right to be homeless must be given at least equal standing with the right of the political community to set standards maintaining the public order. This application of relativism has led to the release of mental patients from confinement and the judicial nullification of most local vagrancy laws.

American education, a field administered almost exclusively by liberal elites, has become a vast laboratory for the implementation of both relativism and equality of result. The predominant moral approach in the public schools was called "value-free" instruction or "values clarification" until the name was de-emphasized after considerable controversy. In his book *The Closing of the American Mind*, University of Chicago professor Allan Bloom wrote that the one strong value held in the 1980s by freshman students from all religious, ethnic, and educational backgrounds was that of "openness"—the idea that all belief systems are relative.

The victory of relativism in elite opinion has not been limited to moral-behavioral issues. It has also affected intellectual standards themselves. One of the earliest strains of 1960s campus activism was a drive against traditional testing and grading. A trend toward "pass-fail" grading proved temporary, but such outgrowths as higher grade averages, relaxed reading requirements, and fewer required courses did not. Meanwhile, in the public schools after the 1960s educational elites became broadly skeptical of various kinds of performance testing.

Intellectual relativism meshes well with the goal of equality of result. A de-emphasis on standardized testing helped make it morally possible to impose affirmative-action quotas benefiting victims of past discrimination. A disbelief in objective standards almost by definition makes the *result* of social policy the only thing that matters.

In due course, relativism and equality of result began to have huge impacts on curricula. At Stanford and many other universities, courses focusing on the study of Western history, thought, and literature were de-emphasized in favor of black studies, feminist studies, native American studies, and the like. The growing Balkanization of curricula resembled nothing so much as the attempt to slice the Democratic party into officially recognized ethnic and gender-based "caucuses" in the period immediately after the McGovern Commission.

In courses where more traditional material was still taught, explicitly relativist instruction and criticism gained ground. In literature, deconstruction taught that language is purely "self-referential," and thus has no universal content or value. In law schools, Critical Legal Studies taught that the making and interpreting of laws is always dependent on the power equation of their time and place. Moral relativism gained almost total sway in seminaries, with the exception of some of those run by evangelical Protestants and Orthodox Jews.

One recent trend on many campuses shows that in the arena where it has greatest sway, liberal relativism is as aggressively committed to standard-setting as its social conservative opponents. This is the widespread enactment of "anti-harassment" standards which punish students for being "verbally aggressive" toward women, gays, and other victims of past discrimination. These standards have proven in practice to be so restrictive that the American Civil Liberties Union—normally a reliable ally of liberalism—has increasingly intervened on behalf of students charged with violating them.

It would seem likely that in some situations relativism or tolerance as the one moral standard could in practice be libertarian or even anarchistic in its implications for society. Where relativism on the part of elites is a derivative of nihilism or apathy, simple permissiveness could easily result. But when it is a derivative of the larger commitment to equality of result, relativism is neither neutral nor benign in its attitude toward those who believe in absolute standards. Outside the campuses, in realms where liberal elites lack the political muscle to impose some version of "political correctness" on its constituency, the elite opinion stream is able to accord very low social status to, say, advocates of community standards restricting pornography.

A New Left proclamation seen in Paris in 1968—"it is forbidden to forbid"—aptly sums up the attitude of liberal elites toward those who would have the community enact standards other than equality of result or relativism. Put another way, if the standard of tolerance and the standard of equality of result ever collide, liberal elites will tend to resolve the conflict in favor of equality. This is logical if, as seems to be the case, equality of result is the governing principle among today's elites and tolerance (equality of all moral values) merely its application to values issues.

It is relativism, nevertheless, not its mother notion of equality of result, that has made enormous inroads in the popular opinion stream. Behavior patterns that fifty years ago were described as "bad," "corrupt," "evil," or "sinful," today are known as "illness," "dependency," "addiction," or "compulsion." As mentioned in Chapter 11, permissiveness has grown steadily in the popular opinion stream on moral-behavioral issues, and if such observers as Bloom are right, the one thing all American secondary education is effectively teaching is a fairly articulate moral and cultural relativism. On abortion, for nearly two decades the central values issue in politics, polls have consistently shown that a significant segment of public opinion believes *both* that abortion is homicide *and* that the decision to abort should be up to the individual. It would seem likely that many of the pivotal voters who believe both these things are influenced by relativism. They have a strong viewpoint of their own, but think it inappropriate to impose it on the community as a whole even in what they believe to be a matter of life and death.

Although relativism among most elites is a subset of equality of result, part of its popular appeal is that it sounds like innate equality—the populist, optimistic vision of people as having an irreducible dignity in the present.

There is no hint of optimism about people in such equality-of-result ideas as mandatory busing, employment quotas, a guaranteed annual income, and punitive tax rates. To one degree or another, they all assume bad motives on the part of the financially successful, indifference by the majority, and near-complete helplessness on the part of society's victims.

In contrast, at least on the surface, relativism seems to be saying that the moral stance of each person has a dignity, and that therefore a decision by society to choose the standards of some people over the standards of others means a loss of dignity by the losers of the debate.

There is some truth to this view, which is why it has popular appeal in the age of equality, and perhaps why some democratic societies such as Sweden appear to have opted for a considerable degree of institutionalized moral relativism. If the rest of the democratic world chooses to follow Sweden's example, then Francis Fukuyama's prediction of the "end of history" could come true in the carefully defined sense he describes. The triumph of democracy would mean the end of serious debate not just about politics but about everything.

The likelier outcome is that politics will still be the unpredictable arena of important decision-making it has always been. The victory of political equality means a proliferation of elites and a more complex menu of choices. It is that very complexity that will tend to drive electorates to make their decisions in terms of organizing principles that sort out and consolidate all the choices. This will mean a drive toward standards, some of which will be strict. Once a democracy chooses a standard that seems to bring goodness or order or beauty to its community life, it will want to enshrine it, to make it permanent and fixed, and even perhaps to communicate it to other cultures.

The widespread acceptance of innate equality has gone a long way toward settling the issue of the political order, which (as much as it has befuddled humanity in the recent transition from monarchy to democracy) is a secondary issue. The primary issue is what people acting together will choose to accomplish.

The United States will almost certainly be the leading indicator. It was the first country to enshrine innate equality as its founding doctrine, and with that head start and the impossibility of a monarchical comeback, it had a long time to experiment with the democratic and populist reforms most of humanity is only starting to play with.

In retrospect, it is not surprising that the success of the black civil rights movement in the early 1960s triggered a values crisis in the United States and arguably all over the world. The ending of legal segregation and the advance of Southern blacks to full status as voters meant that a crucial final stage of political equality had

190 POPULISM AND ELITISM

been achieved in the country that had long been equality's pioneer in the eyes of the world. American elites who were instrumental in that achievement immediately turned their attention to what they saw as logical next steps on equality's road. Even today, they are still sincerely and effectively trying to expand the reach of equality to points where the popular opinion stream has made it clear it has no desire to go. The growing, pervasive assault on traditional values that elites have led is at least in part a reflection of the simple fact that for equality of result to prevail as the community's main value, it must simultaneously pre-empt or marginalize all other values. This it appears to have done in Sweden—a country that combines high taxes and an elaborate welfare net with a near-complete erosion of the traditional family.

The Republican presidential victory of 1968 was fundamentally reactive, without a clear or coherent agenda of its own other than turning back the would-be revolutionaries on the other side. It wouldn't have happened in the way it did, or perhaps at all, without the values crisis among elites which preceded it.

It was not until the 1980s that Ronald Reagan, the most completely populist president since Andrew Jackson, gave Republicans a coherent agenda. But for all his unexpected success in taming inflation, flattening the progressive income tax, and winning the Cold War between democracy and communism, Reagan's administration did nothing to settle the values conflict that had elected Nixon two decades earlier. Throughout the 1980s, liberal elites continued to move forward in making relativism the core of American moral culture.

The ability of the Reagan and Bush administrations to change the federal judiciary has been important, but by itself it can only move politics to a new, more intense stage of a values battle that is already a generation old. On its outcome will hinge the final resolution of split-level realignment, the future shape of both populism and elitism, and almost certainly the agenda of global politics in the age of equality.

ENDNOTES

1. Carl Cohen, "Democracy," in Carl Cohen, ed., *Communism, Fascism, and Democracy* (New York, N.Y.: Random House, 1972), 617–18.
2. Peter F. Drucker, *Men, Ideas & Politics* (New York, N.Y.: Harper Colophon Books, Harper & Row, 1977), 259.
3. Robert Kelley, *The Transatlantic Persuasion: The Liberal-Democratic Mind in the Age of Gladstone* (New York, N.Y.: Alfred A. Knopf, 1969).
4. John Milton Cooper, *The Warrior and the Priest: Woodrow Wilson and Theodore Roosevelt* (Cambridge, Mass.: Belknap Press, Harvard University Press, 1983), 83, 213.
5. Melvin Kranzberg and Joseph Gies, *By the Sweat of Thy Brow: Work in the Western World* (New York, N.Y.: Putnam, 1975), 154, 55.
6. Werner Jaeger, *Paideia: The Ideals of Greek Culture*, Vol. I, 2nd German ed., Gilbert Highet, trans. (New York, N.Y.: A Galaxy Book, Oxford University Press, 1965), 102.
7. John Locke, *The Second Treatise of Government (An Essay Concerning the True Original, Extent and End of Civil Government)* (Oxford: Basil Blackwell, 1966), 106–07; John Dewey, "Democracy and Educational Administration," quoted in Cohen, op. cit., 578; *The Federalist* (New York, N.Y.: Modern Library, Random House, 1937), 338.
8. Robert Kelley, *The Cultural Pattern in American Politics: The First Century* (New York, N.Y.: Alfred A. Knopf, 1979), 265–66.
9. William H. McNeill, *The Shape of European History* (New York, N.Y.: Oxford University Press, 1974), 33n.

10. Ibid., 54.
11. Ibid., 53.
12. Herodotus, *The Persian Wars*, George Rawlinson, trans. (New York, N.Y.: Modern Library, Random House, 1942), 407–08.
13. Quoted in Quentin Skinner, *The Foundations of Modern Political Thought, Vol. I: The Renaissance* (Cambridge, U.K.: Cambridge University Press, 1978), 3.
14. R. K. Webb, "Elizabethans and Puritans," in John A. Garraty and Peter Gay, eds., *The Columbia History of the World* (New York, N.Y.: Harper & Row, 1972), 573.
15. Interview in *Politics Today*, March-April 1980, 49.
16. Jaeger, op. cit., 110.
17. Thomas Paine, *Common Sense and Other Political Writings* (Indianapolis, Ind.: Bobbs-Merrill, 1976), 120.
18. David Spitz, *Patterns of Anti-Democratic Thought* (New York, N.Y.: Free Press, 1965), 148–49.
19. Quoted in *New York Times*, November 26, 1977, 8.
20. Quoted in *TV Guide*, September 4, 1982.
21. Leonard D. White, *The Jeffersonians: A Study in Administrative History, 1801–1829* (New York, N.Y.: Macmillan, 1951), 132.
22. V. O. Key, *Public Opinion and American Democracy* (New York, N.Y.: Alfred A. Knopf, 1961), 553.
23. J. R. Lucas, *The Principles of Politics* (Oxford: Clarendon Press, 1966), 267.
24. Kelley, *The Transatlantic Persuasion*, op. cit., 203.
25. Ibid., 228.
26. Ibid., 209.
27. Benjamin P. Thomas, *Abraham Lincoln* (New York, N.Y.: Alfred A. Knopf, 1952), 499.
28. Letter from 1884 presidential campaign, quoted in Kelley, *The Transatlantic Persuasion*, op. cit., 291.
29. V. O. Key, *The Responsible Electorate: Rationality in Presidential Voting, 1936–60* (Cambridge, Mass.: Belknap Press, Harvard University Press, 1966), 58–59.
30. Alexis de Tocqueville, *The Old Regime and the French Revolution* (Garden City, N.Y.: Doubleday Anchor Books, Doubleday, 1955), 175.
31. James H. Billington, *Fire in the Minds of Men* (New York, N.Y.: Basic Books, 1980), 304–05.

32. Theodore H. White, *The Making of the President 1968* (New York, N.Y.: Atheneum, 1969), 169.
33. Ibid., 136n.
34. James L. Sundquist, *Dynamics of the Party System* (Washington, D.C.: Brookings Institution, 1973).

INDEX